ELVIS

The definitive guide to the king of rock 'n' roll

igloobooks

igloobooks

Written by Kim Aitken

Cover designed by Nicholas Gage
Edited by Natalie Baker

Cover image © Ron Galella / Getty Images
All other images © iStock / Getty images

An imprint of Igloo Books Group,
part of Bonnier Books UK
bonnierbooks.co.uk

Published in 2019
by Igloo Books Ltd, Cottage Farm
Sywell, NN6 0BJ

Manufactured in China. GUA006 1218
10 9 8 7 6 5 4 3 2

Library of Congress Cataloging-in-Publication
Data is available upon request.

ISBN 978-1-4998-8072-4
IglooBooks.com
bonnierbooks.co.uk

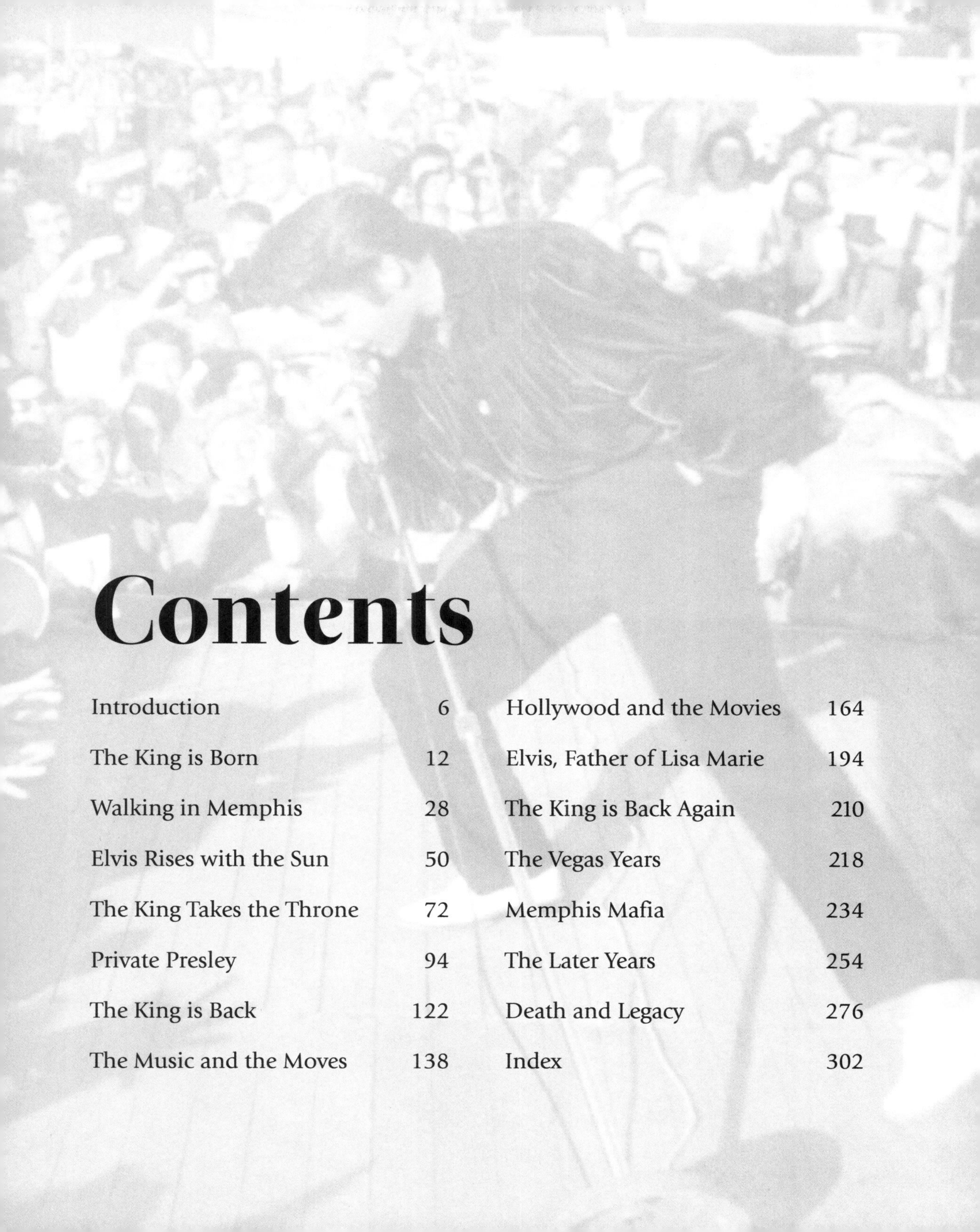

Contents

Elvis performs in concert

Introduction

Born Elvis Presley, dubbed The King of Rock 'n' Roll

Elvis was a fascinating character, a man who came from very humble beginnings in America's South to end up on top of the music world. He died one of the most influential, popular music stars in modern history.

His story began in poverty. Indeed, his psyche was deeply rooted in his upbringing, his world heavily influenced by an overprotective mother and shadowed by the death of his twin brother at birth. His story is not a comfortable, glamorous, or straightforward one.

To explore the life of the hip-shaking teen idol means exploring his early childhood, along with his early musical inspiration and his family life. For while his sex appeal and talent came naturally, his look, his sound, and his image were developed and nurtured from his teenage youth. The influence of musicians and key musical industry players helped to really define his public persona and to cement his status as The King.

Elvis was famous for his iconic quiff

"Ambition is a dream with a V-8 engine."

—Elvis Presley

Elvis's famous hip-shaking moves in Jailhouse Rock

Elvis's career began and ended with music, a sound that represented his soul, his childhood, and the mixed racial and social boundaries of his environment, The King created a new musical sound and genre that would sell over one billion records. No recording artist has matched his achievement since.

Arguably, Elvis still holds the largest number of gold, platinum, and multiplatinum awards in history. In the United States alone, Elvis has had over 150 different albums and singles that have been certified gold, platinum, or multiplatinum by the Recording Industry Association of America (RIAA). He was given fourteen Grammy nominations alone. In addition to such accolades, Elvis has had no less than 149 songs appear on Billboard's Hot 100 Pop Chart in America, with over ninety charted albums and ten of them reaching Number One status in the US.

Blessed with movie-star looks, he also starred in thirty-three films and was the first popular music artist to move to the big screen with commercial success.

His romantic life was always complicated. It has been said that from his youth he met and held several girlfriends at the same time. Elvis famously went on to choose a virgin bride and became a husband and a father, although neither of these roles was conventional for Elvis in any way.

His later years were more difficult for his fans and audiences to digest, and for many the Las Vegas years signaled the decline of Elvis's musical credibility, looks, and health. Regardless, his live shows were regular sellouts and continue to live on today through Elvis impersonators—whose performances also sell out, over forty years since his death.

Despite the debate regarding this legacy, Elvis's popularity cannot be challenged. Blending incredible talent, sex appeal, good looks, and plenty of personality, Elvis charmed millions and continues to inspire new generations of musicians and stars.

His life, loves, and career are legendary.

Elvis performing in his later years

Elvis performing live at the Nassau Coliseum, 1975

The King is Born

Elvis Presley was born and raised in poor Mississippi

The King of Rock 'n' Roll was born just before dawn on January 8, 1935 in a tiny, two-room house located in a poor neighborhood of Mississippi called East Tupelo. A "shotgun house," the style of which represented poor America, theirs was without electricity and indoor plumbing, built by his father, grandfather, and uncle.

Named Elvis Aron (later changed to Aaron) Presley, he was delivered a little over half an hour after his identical twin brother Jesse Garon, who was sadly stillborn. He was to be an only child, raised by young parents who relied on the help of family and welfare to pay for food and basic provisions—even items like diapers were kindly donated by neighbors.

The fact that Elvis was born in an own-built "shotgun house," and came from nothing was symbolic of the birth and growth of his musical career.

His father told an interviewer, Sidney Fields, when Elvis became famous:

"We were poor. When I was sick my wife walked to work many times because she had no carfare. And many times we hardly had any lunch money to give Elvis. But we did eat and had clothes and a roof over our heads. Maybe we got them all on credit, but we had them. We never had much until three years ago, but Elvis never wanted for anything even when we were troubled."

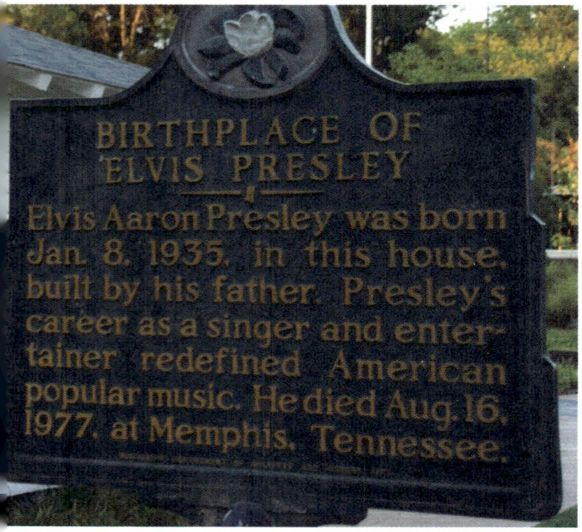

Birthplace sign of Elvis Presley, Tupelo, Mississippi, USA

"When I was a child, ladies and gentlemen, I was a dreamer. I read comic books, and I was the hero of the comic book. I saw movies and I was the hero in the movie. So every dream I ever dreamed, has come true a hundred times. . . ."

—Elvis, in his acceptance speech for the 1970 Ten Outstanding Young Men of the Nation Award, January 16, 1971

Elvis Presley (1945) standing between his parents outside of their home in Tupelo, Mississippi.

Elvis's father, Vernon, was only eighteen when Elvis was born, and struggled to make ends meet. When Elvis was just three years old, Vernon was found guilty of forging a check made out to him for the sale of a pig. After Vernon was jailed for eight months, he was unable to make repayments and lost the house, forcing Elvis and his twenty-two-year-old mother Gladys to move in with relatives.

Elvis was devastated by his father's departure, and locals recalled the young boy would sit on the porch crying, wailing for his daddy.

Perhaps because of this misfortune early in life, Elvis and his mother formed an unusually close bond. She was described as overprotective of her only son. Elvis later told an interviewer, "My mama never let me out of her sight. I couldn't go down to the creek with the other kids."

When the interviewer Sidney Fields wrote up his story to accompany the interview in the *Daily Mirror*, he said of Elvis's parents, "I like these people. They're simple, neighborly, unaffected by the fame and fortune of their son, or the furor he has created."

According to his mother in this same interview after her son's success, she said Elvis was always concerned about his mother and father. When Elvis was only five years old, he watched his father help a neighbor put a fire out in their house. He screamed for his daddy. "He was afraid his father wouldn't ever come out," said his mother. "I just told him, 'Daddy will be all right, now. You stop that, hear!' And he did."

Two-year-old Elvis Presley poses for a family portrait with his parents Gladys Presley and Vernon Presley in 1937

Birthplace of Elvis Presley, Tupelo, Mississippi, USA

Equally, his parents worried about him and said they asked him to stop playing football after learning that one young boy had died from a blood clot as a result of playing a game. In the interview Vernon said, "That scared both of us and we made Elvis quit."

Elvis's unique physical beauty was the result of his mixed ancestry. His seamstress mother was of Scottish, Irish, and Native American Cherokee descent, his father from Scottish and German origin. Early childhood photos show Elvis's lopsided cheeky grin and warm skin tone, with dark eyes and blond hair. He was an unconventionally good-looking boy and would grow up to become a desirable, handsome rock star.

Despite his good looks, Elvis was not a popular child. His first school—East Tupelo Consolidated—recorded average academic results and his peers regarded him as a bit of a loner.

Elvis was raised a Christian, attending church for the First Assembly of God. His mother and father had met at the church and the family would continue to attend there. While Elvis would later question his faith, his church attendance helped further nurture his belief in music.

Elvis was, as his classmates noticed, shy and a loner. He escaped into the fantasy world of comic books, his favorite being *Captain Marvel, Jr.* Although he would swap comics with other kids, his social interaction was limited.

It was his love of country music that first got him noticed as a youngster.

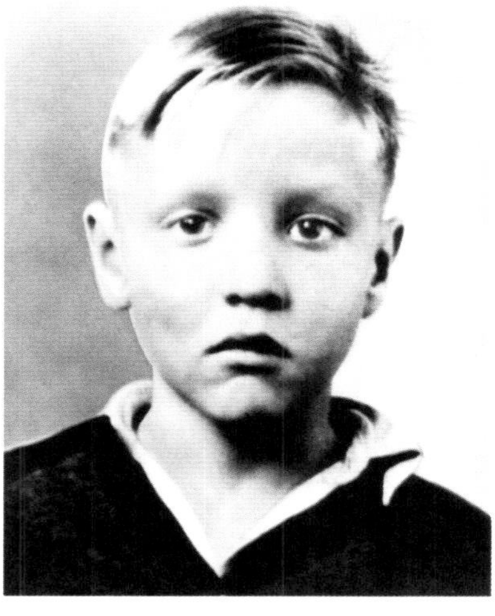

Elvis Presley as a child

Elvis Presley with radio DJ and high school classmate George Klein in December, 1970

Elvis Presley's first guitar

In the first term of his first year at school, Elvis's teacher asked her class if any of the students would like to say a prayer. Instead of saying a prayer, Elvis stood up and sang Red Foley's "Old Shep." The teacher took Elvis to the school principal, who was also impressed by his singing.

Elvis was then asked to sing in a contest at the Mississippi-Alabama Fair and Dairy Show in 1945, which was broadcast on the local radio. Coming in a mere fifth, Elvis's talent was yet to be recognized and nurtured.

Elvis's father recalled, "At nine he was picked to sing alone in church. At home we sang as a trio, when Gladys wasn't playin' the harmonica. Elvis always had a natural talent. He can't read a note even now. But you don't have to teach a fish to swim." A year later, at age ten, with frequent home moves around Tupelo, Elvis ended up attending a new school in sixth grade, Milam Junior High, where he was also described as a loner. He was teased for being "white trash" and the children made fun of him singing hillbilly songs.

Many accounts of Elvis's childhood from sources who knew him say he was a sweet boy, who never really fit in. He was also described by other accounts as a lovable rogue or misfit.

His tenth year was also the year he was given his first guitar (accounts differ, with some recalling it was his twelfth birthday). Some also report Elvis wanted a bicycle, while others claim he wanted a shotgun. Regardless, the $6.95 guitar was his birthday gift.

"I took the guitar, and I watched people, and I learned to play a little bit. But I would never sing in public. I was very shy about it."

—Elvis Presley

Elvis Presley wearing his high school Army uniform in 1955

Elvis Presley
On Louisiana
Hayride, *1954*

Another home move later, Elvis was living in a largely African-American neighborhood, nicknamed "Shake Rag." He became strongly influenced by a hillbilly singer called Mississippi Slim and gospel music.

Slim held a spot on the Tupelo radio station, WELO. Elvis was obsessed. Slim's younger brother attended school with Elvis and helped him progress his talent by bringing him into the radio station, even tutoring him on guitar and teaching chord techniques.

When Elvis turned twelve, Slim scheduled him for two live performances at WELO. The first one was a disaster, with Elvis overcome by nerves; he did not even begin the performance. Fortunately, the second opportunity was fulfilled and Elvis gave his first radio performance at just twelve years of age.

In 1948, when Elvis was in eighth grade, the family moved again. This time, the Presleys moved out of Tupelo to Memphis, Tennessee. Still a low-income family, they moved into a two-bedroom apartment in a public housing complex.

According to his parents, Elvis skipped the first day of high school out of fear of being disliked. His father said he always wanted to be liked, "And when he isn't, he worries about it."

He continued to be bullied by his classmates, perceived as a "mama's boy."

Ironically, Elvis was awarded only a grade C in music at this time. In fact, his teacher told him he had no aptitude for singing.

His shyness for singing publicly continued through his teenage years.

"I never expected to be anybody important."

—Elvis Presley

A young Elvis performing in 1954

It was during his junior year, however, that he started to receive more and more attention. A self-styled, good-looking young man, Elvis greased his hair, grew sideburns, and wore dress pants instead of jeans. Fashion conscious from a young age, Elvis tried to emulate his film heroes James Dean and Marlon Brando.

He shopped on Beale Street and frequented the Beale Street gigs, where the blues scene in Memphis was burgeoning.

Elvis's clothes shopping trips were funded by the various jobs he held in his teen years: at the local cinema, Loew's, and at Precision Tools.

His mother recalled a teenage Elvis helping out with money: "And even when he was in school he'd go around and pay the grocery bill, $25, $30. We didn't ask him to. He'd just do it himself."

Elvis was also a serious romantic, and having fallen in love at thirteen with a girl from church, Magdaline Morgan, he secretly made a marriage license for them, copied from his parents' certificate. According to reports, even Magdaline herself was not aware of this until after his death.

Family photo from 1954

Elvis Presley poses for a portrait in 1954

His father recalled he had girlfriends since he was eleven, but that "He didn't have real dates till then . . . Once, when he was sixteen, I seen him sittin' real close to a little girl and I spoke to him about what he should know. He listened. He always does. We've been lucky. All the girls he's known have been nice kids."

In his senior year of high school in 1953, he finally overcame his performance anxiety and readied himself for a show. Playing guitar, Elvis sang Teresa Brewer's hit "Till I Waltz Again With You" and suddenly his popularity soared:

"I wasn't popular in school . . . I failed music—only thing I ever failed. And then they entered me in this talent show . . . when I came onstage I heard people kind of rumbling and whispering and so forth, 'cause nobody knew I even sang. It was amazing how popular I became after that."
—Elvis Presley

Elvis graduated from high school that year.

Elvis in the classroom

High school prom date of Elvis Presley (right) and Regis Wilson Vaughn (left) in 1953

Home of the Mississippi Blues Festival

Memphis blues scene where Elvis first discovered his love for the genre

Walking in Memphis

Elvis's early musical influences and the blues scene in Memphis

Like Elvis's poor upbringing, the musicians who played the blues came from the poor South.

Originating in the early 1900s, the Memphis blues genre was used to describe the mood of musicians playing vaudeville shows along the Mississippi River and Delta. The man credited with establishing the blues was a band man named W.C. Handy, who was inspired to write a song in the genre when he heard a man singing a slow, sad song while playing a guitar by sliding a knife along the strings.

African-Americans who had left the Mississippi Delta and other poor, southern areas were moved by this burgeoning Memphis blues scene, which culminated in the Beale Street district of downtown Memphis. Running from the Mississippi River down to East Street, Beale Street was (and is still today) nearly two miles of blues clubs and restaurants, and is steeped in musical and cultural history.

The street was originally an avenue where trade merchants sold goods, and in the late 1800s traveling musicians would perform along the street. After yellow fever hit the area, the city had to forfeit its charter. The South's first black millionaire, Robert Church, purchased land around the street, proceeding to renovate and nurture it into a cultural district.

Famous blues musicians like Muddy Waters played on Beale Street

Beale Street became the place to be for African-Americans. With a large, mostly affluent black population, Memphis was then the largest city along the Mississippi river. In the period before the Great Depression, records released from Memphis Blues performers regularly sold more than the other blues genres. Different from the Chicago Blues, which featured more electric guitar, the Delta Blues showcased acoustic guitar and wailing harmonicas. In particular, the slide guitar marks the sound of the Delta and Memphis Blues.

The Memphis music scene grew from the blues genre that evolved post-Civil War. It represented sadness, hardship, tough living, love, and romance. With its moody atmosphere and obsession with music, many have described Memphis as "home of the blues."

During the 1930s, amplified guitar pickups helped progress the sound of the Memphis Blues. Later, famous blues musicians, including Louis Armstrong, B.B. King, Muddy Waters, and Rufus Thomas performed on Beale Street, further developing the style dubbed the Memphis Blues.

B.B. King, another musician to heavily influence Elvis

Louis Armstrong was a regular player on Beale Street

LOANS
MORRIS LIPPMAN

Beale Street circa 1935 in Memphis, Tennessee

Beale Street in Memphis is jammed with clubs, bars, restaurants, and music shops

Memphis was certainly home to Elvis's musical beginnings. By the time Elvis was of age to experience Beale Street, some of the nightlife was seedy and boozy, with wailing music heard inside and outside venues.

Even though it was a place where black and white could mix and socialize without judgment or intimidation, Elvis was one of few white people visiting Beale Street. Elvis, along with the thousands of visitors each night, could see blues legends perform, along with street artists while walking home.

The fact that Elvis and Memphis are now synonymous with each other is no surprise.

In Memphis, Elvis had access to not just radio, record stores, and church music, he also soaked up music in nightclubs on Beale Street and played in a band with other boys from the housing complex in which he lived.

Elvis gets a parking ticket on Beale Street, 1956

MALCO

The thriving music scene in the Beale Street haunts, downtown Memphis, were home to black blues and rhythm and blues artists. Elvis was a fan. He would watch acts like Big Memphis Ma Rainey and Rufus Thomas. According to Calvin Newborn, a well-known artist of the time, Elvis also listened to his performances and ended up taking some advice on guitar style and lessons.

Interestingly, B.B. King recalls knowing the other King from frequenting the music events on Beale Street in Memphis, long before Elvis became a famous singer.

"I remember Elvis as a young man hanging around the Sun studios. Even then, I knew this kid had a tremendous talent. He was a dynamic young boy. His phraseology, his way of looking at a song, was as unique as Sinatra's. I was a tremendous fan, and had Elvis lived, there would have been no end to his inventiveness."
—B.B. King

B.B. King became a big Elvis fan

Rufus Thomas's style was a big influence on a young Elvis

Elvis is widely credited with promoting the popularity of the rockabilly style

The romantic, poor Tupelo kid in Elvis must have identified with the music and, in particular, the messages from the blues. Such freedom of expression and emotive, heartfelt music must have made an impression on the teenage Elvis.

It is perhaps no surprise then that the singer Joe Cocker later described Elvis as "the greatest white blues singer in the world."

To listen to singles such as "Hound Dog," "Reconsider Baby," "Stranger in My Own Home Town," "That's All Right (Mama)" "Mystery Train," and "Good Rockin' Tonight" is to listen to the blues, albeit Elvis's white version of the blues.

These blues influences certainly helped shape his style—later to be described by many as "rockabilly." While he did not necessarily "invent" rockabilly, he is widely credited with making it popular by bringing it to the masses, with his own unique twist. In doing so, he also brought social and civil rights to the consciousness of the masses.

Elvis was a great supporter of the civil rights movement

Little Richard credited Elvis with introducing black music to the masses

While many later complained that Elvis took his experiences from Memphis and became "the white boy who stole the blues," it is much more likely that he was simply and unconditionally moved and inspired by them.

As the performer Little Richard stated, "He was an integrator. Elvis was a blessing. They wouldn't let black music through, but he opened the door."

To hear Elvis's style is to also hear the influence of Big Mama Thornton, Arthur "Big Boy" Crudup, The Prisonaires, Lowell Fulson, Chuck Berry, Bo Diddley, Little Richard, and Fats Domino.

Elvis identified with the rhythm and blues genre: he felt the blues.

Elvis was a big fan of Fats Domino

"Rhythm is something you either have or don't have, but when you have it, you have it all over."

—Elvis Presley

Lowell Fulson's style influenced a young Elvis

It seems Elvis took his love of church gospel, country, and western music from his early childhood, and added the black rhythm and blues genre he loved from those Memphis teen years. The fusion of these styles, along with the influence of popular music he heard on radio and in the record stores, helped him to create his own unique style.

Self-taught, Elvis's musical ability grew and grew during his teenage years. In addition to his time on Beale Street, he spent the rest of his spare time in record stores and was a regular at gospel singing nights.

Elvis developed a love for gospel music from his childhood

Elvis in the studio in the mid-1950s

Memphis was the epicenter of white gospel music in the 50s and Elvis adored the four-part harmonies of quartets like those at the monthly All-Night Singings he attended downtown. They played a large part in Elvis's musical education, and he would continue to attend the gospel sings at the Ellis Auditorium with his girlfriend long after he attended as a youth with his parents.

But his passion was first cultivated and nurtured in the gospel choir sounds heard at the First Assembly of God church he had regularly attended with his parents as a youngster. From the age of two, Elvis would display a curiosity for music and singing. His mother recalled, "He would slide down off my lap, run into the aisle, and scramble up to the platform. There he would stand looking at the choir and trying to sing with them."

An old wooden church in Mississippi, the type Elvis would have attended

Elvis playing to one of his first audiences in the early 1950s

Elvis's music is often discussed in the context of gospel, and having won awards and recognition in gospel sound, is widely acknowledged as a key genre in his music.

His country music sound, however, was less publicized and recognized. The country fraternity, however, eagerly recognize Elvis's influence by and for the genre. In more recent years, especially so—he was inducted to the Country Music Hall of Fame in 1998.

It is now mostly accepted that he did fuse the country sound with rhythm and blues, In fact, he was successful in the country market first and, interestingly, very quickly. Perhaps because of his appeal with younger listeners, Elvis received great exposure on country radio, played by country disc jockeys (DJs). His notoriety and rising success can be traced back to this country market.

Country Music Hall of Fame Museum, Nashville, Tennessee

Elvis enjoyed the sounds of the Delta Rhythm Boys

CBS

AMPEX

Elvis Presley poses with record producer Sam Phillips, Leo Soroka, and Robert Johnson at Sun Recording Studios in Memphis, Tennessee

Sam Phillips also discovered Johnny Cash

Elvis Rises with the Sun

Discovering his sound with Sun Records and Sam Phillips

While Elvis was busy discovering the sights and sounds of the Memphis Blues scene down on Beale Street, another music lover was determined to bring his passion for the blues to the masses.

Sam Phillips was destined to be the man who invented rock 'n' roll. As the founder of Sun Records, he is credited with helping a young Elvis with discovering his persona as the King of Rock 'n' Roll.

"If you're not doing something different, you're not doing anything."
—Sam Phillips

In the 1940s and 1950s Phillips was a producer, DJ, and talent scout who famously discovered talents such as Johnny Cash and Jerry Lee Lewis. He launched Elvis's career in 1954.

To understand Phillips's unique relationship with Elvis requires an understanding of their commonality. Sam Phillips was born in Alabama, the youngest of eight children, and after his father's death while he was in high school, was forced to drop out and support his mother and deaf-mute aunt. Like Elvis, he experienced a poor upbringing and hardship early in his life.

"I was training to be an electrician. I suppose I got wired the wrong way round somewhere along the line."

—Elvis Presley

Sam Phillips at Sun Records, 1960

And like Elvis, Phillips developed a keen interest in music saying, "music moves the soul."

In high school, he played the sousaphone, trombone and drums, and reportedly also led a seventy-two-piece strong marching band.

After Phillips was married and settled with children, he took a job hosting the local radio station Elvis listened to in Memphis. He said he immediately fell in love with Beale Street and the atmosphere there.

Setting up a modest studio, Phillips opened Sun Records and went on to famously sign artists like B.B. King and Roy Orbison.

Originally, his studio was set up in a small storefront on Union Avenue rented for $150 a month. He also installed recording equipment and called it the Memphis Recording Service, which was designed and marketed for music, weddings, funerals, and the like. The business advertised, "We record anything, anywhere, anytime."

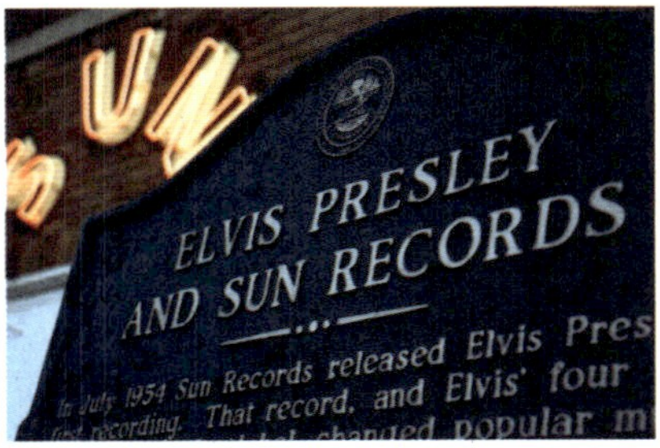

Sun Studio became known as the "Birthplace of Rock 'n' Roll"

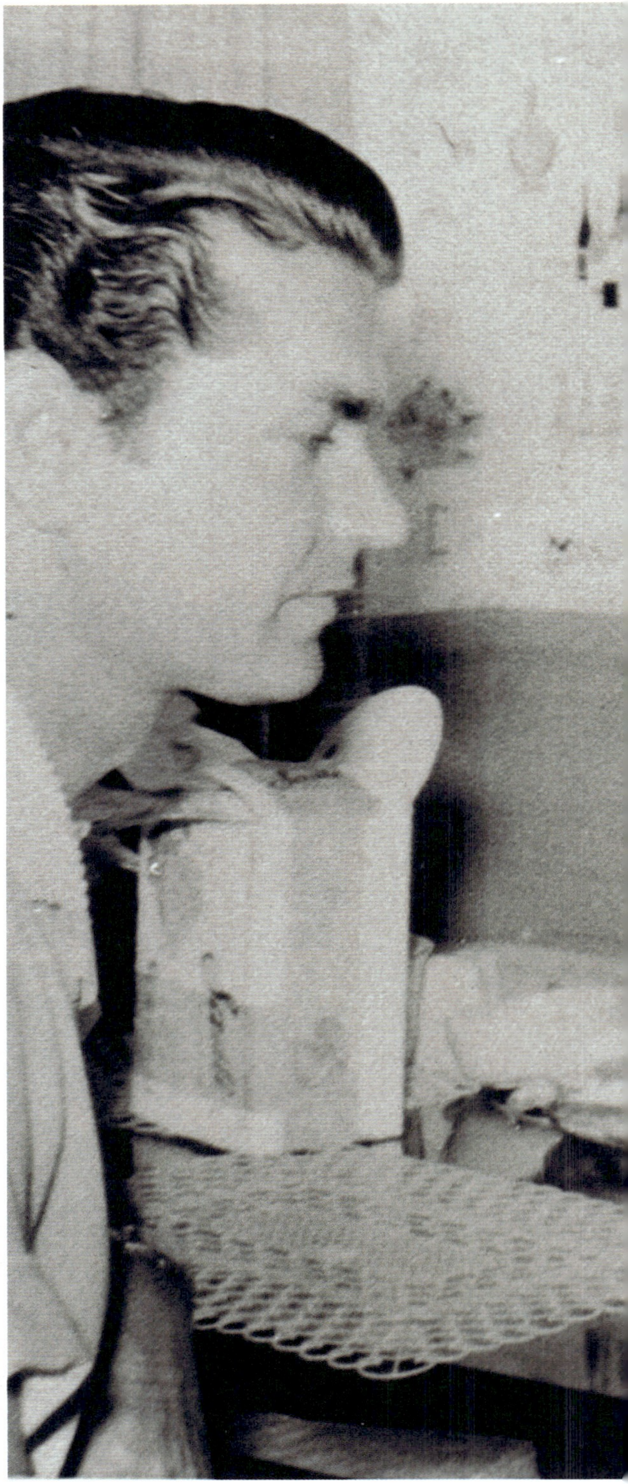

Elvis Presley and Sam Phillips eating ice cream and cake in 1956

Phillips denied reports that he had repeatedly said he could "make a million dollars if he could find a white man who sang black rhythms with a black feel."

Much later, in 1978, Phillips told a reporter with the *New York Times*, "That quote is an injustice both to the whites and the blacks. I was trying to establish an identity in music, and black and white had nothing to do with it."

With his poor upbringing during the depression, Phillips identified with the performers he had recording in his studios—he could relate to them and bring out the best in them. He told the *Dallas Morning News* that his aim was to record "the real gutbucket stuff that other labels weren't putting out."

Sun Studios—now an iconic landmark in Tennessee

Elvis Presley performs onstage with a new guitar in 1955

In the summer of 1953, a young Elvis walked into the Sun Records studio at 706 Union Avenue, in downtown Memphis. He was there to use the DIY record-making facility called the Memphis Recording Service. By some accounts, he was there to record some songs for his mother.

Financially, Phillips and Sun Records were struggling. When eighteen-year-old Elvis came in, it was perfect timing.

Phillips thought that Presley was an introverted man, according to reports. Nonetheless, Phillips said:

"After listening to his voice, seeing his demeanor . . . and what I thought was a very different style . . . I was highly impressed with what I thought he could do as an artist."

—Sam Phillips, in a recorded interview on Elvis April 7, 1992

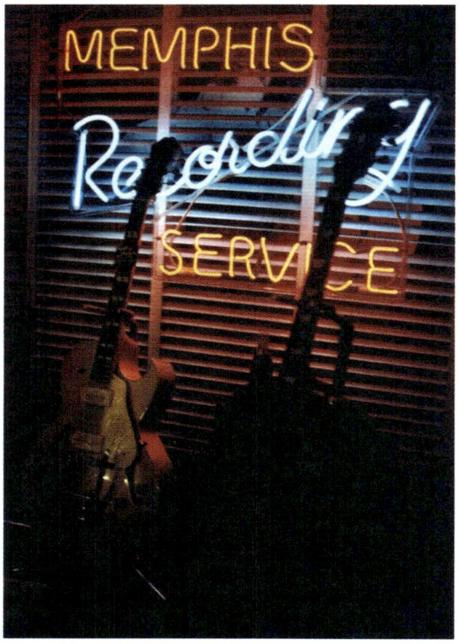

The self-recording service advertised at Sun Studios

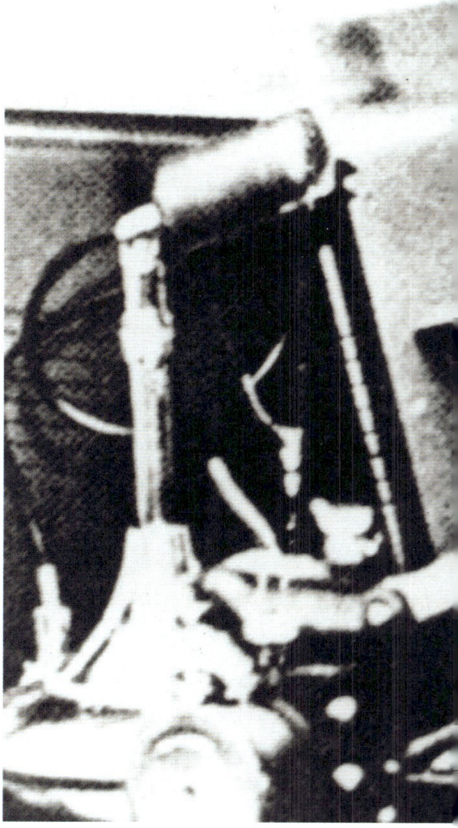

Left–right; Elvis Presley, Bill Black, Scotty Moore, Sam Phillips in the Sun Records studio

"When Elvis came in and he performed those first two songs, I was blown away by this guy's talent. By that I don't mean that I heard the finished thing, but I just heard some instinctive things about this person's intonations and stuff.

"Of course, we didn't talk about 'intonations' and all of that jazz, but that's what I was hearing and feeling! You know, that's how you communicate, and so it didn't take a genius to recognize that this person Elvis had real potential.

"My honest opinion was that he might be that white guy who could get the overtones and the sexual feel in there without anything being vulgar; just that actual thing that gets hold of somebody and says, 'Hey, listen to me!'"

—Sam Phillips, For Elvis Fans Only, August 2, 2004

Although Phillips noticed The King's voice and charisma as he recorded versions of "My Happiness" and "That's When Your Heartache Begins" for a $3.98 fee, it would be another year before they would begin to work together.

Elvis cashing one of his first checks in 1956

Elvis recording and playing at RCA

Elvis performing with Scotty Moore on a brand-new guitar

Bill Black, the bass player with Elvis Presley

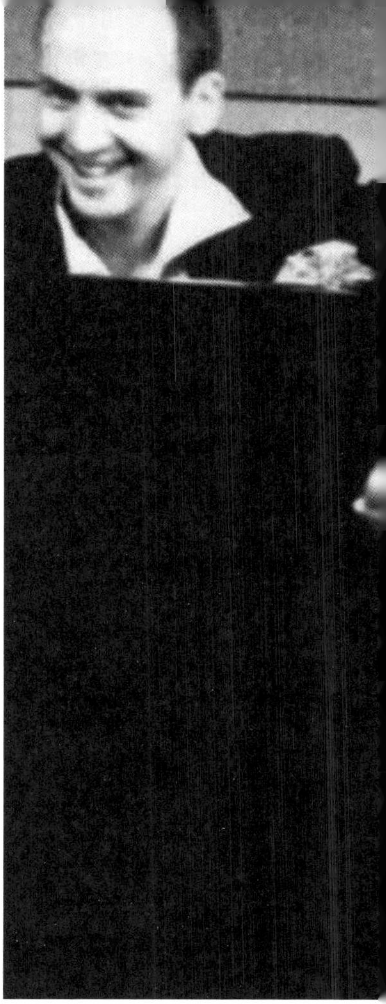

Scotty Moore on the set of Jailhouse Rock

It was reported that Phillips had so many other artists consuming his time and attention that he struggled to focus on Elvis right away. Some other accounts suggest that Phillips was not actually in the studio at the time, and only heard his second recording in the new year of 1954. At this time, Elvis was working as a driver for Crown Electric Company and studying at night school to be an electrician.

During the summer of 1954, at the suggestion of his studio assistant, Marion Keisker, Phillips invited Elvis into the studio. Keisker recalled asking Elvis what his singing was like and he replied, "I sing all kinds," and "I don't sound like nobody." Her notes on his session read, "Good ballad singer. Hold."

There was no real method to their approach; it was about trying out different arrangements until they discovered the right sound. At first, Phillips was not impressed with how Elvis delivered the songs he requested. After asking him to sing some pop songs of the time in his own way, Phillips decided there was something about Elvis, but with bassist Bill Black and guitarist Scotty Moore, who were in a country and western outfit called Starlight Wranglers, working on material and experimenting with sounds. Some sources recall the three rehearsed for months before recording in the studio.

Left–right; Scotty Moore, Elvis Presley, and Bill Black

Elvis did not actually have a band at the time—it was Phillips who introduced Black and Moore, and decided to shape Elvis's voice and rhythm guitar sound. With his guidance, Elvis learned production qualities and the "feel" that Phillips described when they happened on a perfect cut.

Phillips's ear was good. He could recognize a unique sound that would sell—and finally they came up with "That's All Right (Mama)."

It happened just at the last minute.

Phillips recalled they had started packing down the instruments to close a long, tedious session one evening, July 5, to the point where the door to the studio was open and everyone was ready to leave. Elvis started on his rhythm guitar singing from Arthur Crudup's 1946 blues hit "That's All Right . . ." and Phillips froze.

Elvis's first single, That's All Right (Mama)

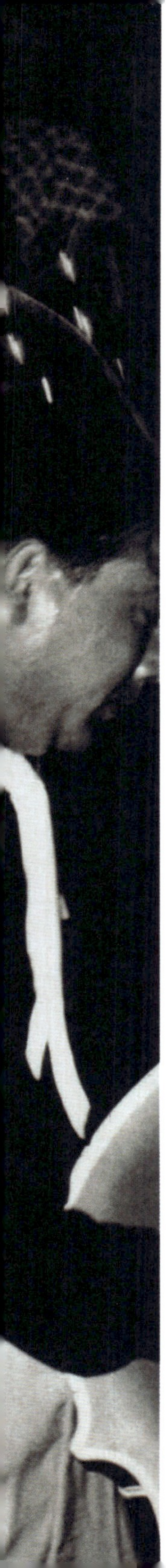

Elvis Presley performs onstage with his brand-new Martin D-28 acoustic guitar on July 31, 1955

"There was no question in my mind. That was the sound, the feel, even the tempo."

—Sam Phillips, For Elvis Fans Only, August 2, 2004

With a fast rhythm and no drums, the bass going fast to keep time with his vocals, guitar wailing in and out, Phillips asked what they were doing. They apparently said they didn't know.

"Well, back it up, try to find a place to start, and do it again," Phillips said.

A maximum of four takes later the single was ready. Just days later, the Memphis DJ Dewey Phillips played the song on his radio show and listeners phoned in to ask who it was singing. He ended up playing the record over and over that same show. Some reports indicate Elvis was invited in for an interview that night, too. Rock 'n' Roll was born.

Elvis Presley joins his guitar player Scotty Moore (left) and bass player Bill Black (right) on a weekly broadcast of Louisiana Hayride *at the Shreveport Auditorium*

Dewey Phillips promoted Elvis's music on air

WHBQ

Elvis wanted to sing like Dean Martin

Phillips was innovative for his time, using new techniques like pulling back on the volume of the vocals to blend with the instruments of the band and introducing an echo on the vocals, achieved by running the tape through a second recorder head.

Phillips knew Elvis before the fame, the hip-swiveling controversy, and the Vegas years. He helped shaped the future King of Rock 'n' Roll by encouraging him to be raw and very unlike the man Elvis wanted to sing like—Dean Martin.

Steering Elvis away from a crooner style and toward the rockabilly, bluesy, and raw Elvis that was recorded on the single "That's All Right (Mama)" Phillips launched the career of the newest sounding singer—with a genre all of his own.

"Elvis had sex written all over him from the day he walked in the door. I don't mean anything about him being good-looking, because he really wasn't as good-looking as he would develop a little later on, but he had sex written all over him, and the right kind," said Phillips.

"When this man opened his mouth it had sex, when you saw him onstage you couldn't take your eyes off him, and that was even as a male. I don't want to use the word 'charisma', but this guy—and I'm talking about him in a total, total personal way, in addition to fantastic talent as far as his singing was concerned—had a certain ability for contact, and to a measured degree he could give you that sexual feel, or whatever feel was needed, if a song indicated that it had that potential."

Elvis performing at an intimate gig in 1956

Phillips later said there was something in Elvis's soul and his spirit, to survive the entertainment business and all the years of commentary at such a phenomenal, global level. And he certainly was granted a background at Sun Records that gave him the "inertia" to feel confidence in himself and his ability.

Despite popularity and notoriety, the Sun label was not performing well financially. A practical businessman, Phillips ended up selling Elvis's contract to RCA Records for a whopping $35,000, which was at the time, unheard of.

Sam Phillips may not have made the biggest or best investment in Elvis, who would go on to become worth around $7 million annually at the height of his fame, however he is largely recognized as being the legend who discovered Elvis. He used the money from selling the contract to develop other musicians and hits, including Perkins' hit "Blue Suede Shoes."

In *Last Train to Memphis: The Rise of Elvis Presley*, author and biographer Peter Guralnick said Phillips's accomplishment was recognizing "the unlimited possibilities, and untapped potential, in the popular appetite for African-American culture."

He was inducted into the Rock 'n' Roll Hall of Fame in 1986. The Sun Records studio is now a tourist attraction and was named a National Historic Landmark.

Recording at RCA again in 1956

Elvis records the soundtrack for his film Love Me Tender

The King Takes the Throne

Elvis's meteoric rise to success

Following the great chemistry Elvis had with Black and Moore at the 1954 recording, The King happened on his first local hit song. Moore became his manager and local shows soon followed.

Later that same year, happening country radio show *Louisiana Hayride* invited Elvis to appear. He also made it onto local television some six months after, and a few more of his recorded singles "Good Rockin' Tonight," and "I Don't Care if the Sun Don't Shine" increased his popularity in Memphis. During this period, Presley hired a new manager in the local DJ Bob Neal. Neal encouraged Elvis to audition for a talent show in New York, although he did not win the hearts of judges.

The judges must have later questioned their scouting abilities, considering it was only a few months later that an Elvis gig in Florida started a riot.

Still only a local country act, Elvis received his first Number One record, with his adaptation of Junior Parker's "Mystery Train," in September of 1954. His ascent to fame and stardom was quick, taking a little under a year from his first recording to his first Number One.

It was around this time that Elvis was getting more attention from music promoter Colonel Tom Parker, who had met him through Neal. Parker started to get more involved in Elvis's career and by the time Sun Records had sold his contract to RCA, Parker was also getting his connections in the music publishing arena involved.

When the contract went through, Elvis used his $5,000 advance to buy his mother a pink Cadillac, as he'd promised her as a young boy.

In 1956, Parker signed Elvis to a manager's contract, which allowed him 25 percent of the star's earnings. The contract held firm right up to Elvis's death and to royalties and estate earnings long after his passing.

Elvis with manager, Colonel Tom Parker

Elvis on the Louisiana Hayride *tour*

Elvis Presley performing on The Milton Berle Show *in Burbank, California on June 4, 1956*

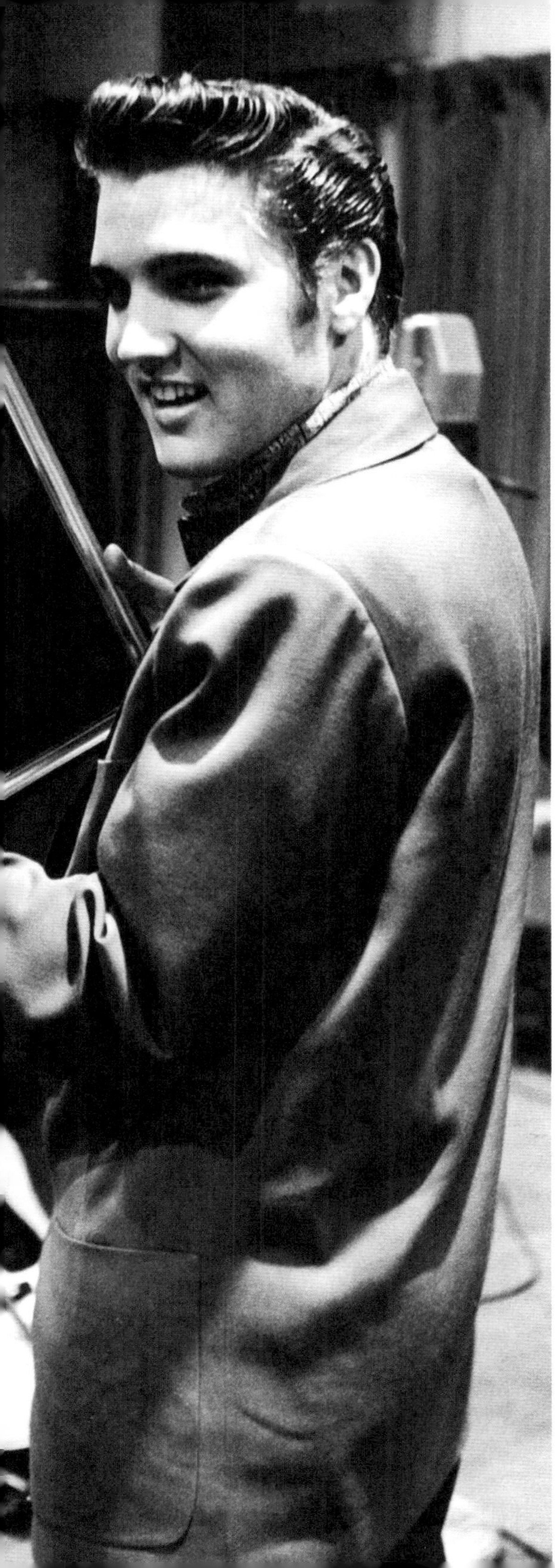

Despite this outrageously generous cut (the standard was 10 percent), Parker was good for Elvis's rise to rock stardom. Parker managed him through his first record for RCA and his national television appearance on *Stage Show*, a popular program hosted by the Dorsey Brothers, Tommy and Jimmy, who were big band members. Elvis then followed with another six appearances on the same show.

Under Parker's wing, Elvis went on to perform on the Ed Sullivan, Milton Berle, and Steve Allen shows, all popular in their own right.

Parker set up the first recording with RCA in Nashville, in January, with the usual Black and Moore support. He also added the pianist Floyd Cramer and guitarist Chet Atkins, plus three backup singers, for fuller sound. What followed was "Heartbreak Hotel," the single that gave Parker leverage to secure Elvis on national TV with channel CBS. "Heartbreak Hotel" became his first Number One pop song.

Following filming at CBS in New York, Elvis recorded a further eight tracks in the RCA studios of the Big Apple. This recording included "Blue Suede Shoes," a famous and extremely popular song of The King's.

In March, RCA released Elvis's self-titled debut album. It included five songs from unreleased material at Sun Studios. They completed the mixed menu of the album, as there were two country songs and one pop song to complement the rock 'n' roll feel of the other tracks. It was not only the first rock 'n' roll album to get to Number One on Billboard's chart, but stayed at the top for ten weeks.

Elvis Presley holding framed gold record of "Heartbreak Hotel"

A publicity shot for Love Me Tender, *1956*

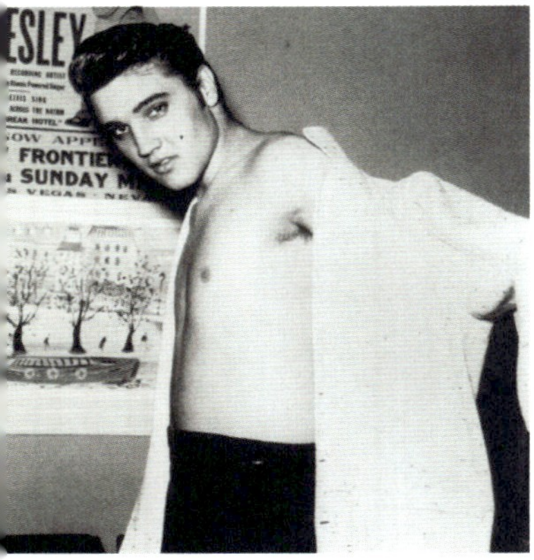

Elvis in front of a poster for his Las Vegas show

By April, national TV station NBC had Elvis on its *The Milton Berle Show*. It was well received. Just a short time later, Elvis had a scare.

Taking a flight back to Nashville, Elvis and his bandmates were left extremely unsettled after the engine failed and the plane nearly went down.

Just as Elvis seemed to have many lives, so he had many hits to come.

And while many assume that Elvis's Las Vegas career began much later, in fact he had tested the waters with performances in Vegas at this early point in his career. Parker had Elvis on The Strip for two weeks, performing to a lackluster audience of middle-aged folk. They were not his target audience.

Following this, he started a tour of the American midwest, with fifteen cities in fifteen days. It was on this tour that Elvis began featuring a cover of Big Mama Thorton's "Hound Dog" as part of his closing act.

His popularity was reaching fever pitch.

Alongside his television appearances, in the middle of the year Elvis was contracted to shoot his first film, *Love Me Tender*. Costing £1,000,000 to make, and released a short three months after filming began, it only took three days to break even. Elvis was so watchable, be it singing or acting, audiences could not get enough of him. He signed with Paramount Pictures for a seven-year movie contract.

After all of the success and attention that followed *The Milton Berle Show*, and of course the excellent TV ratings, it should have come as no surprise that Steve Allen and Ed Sullivan were to follow. National television channel giant NBC booked Elvis to appear on Steve Allen, filmed in New York that July.

Movie art for the film Love Me Tender, *1956*

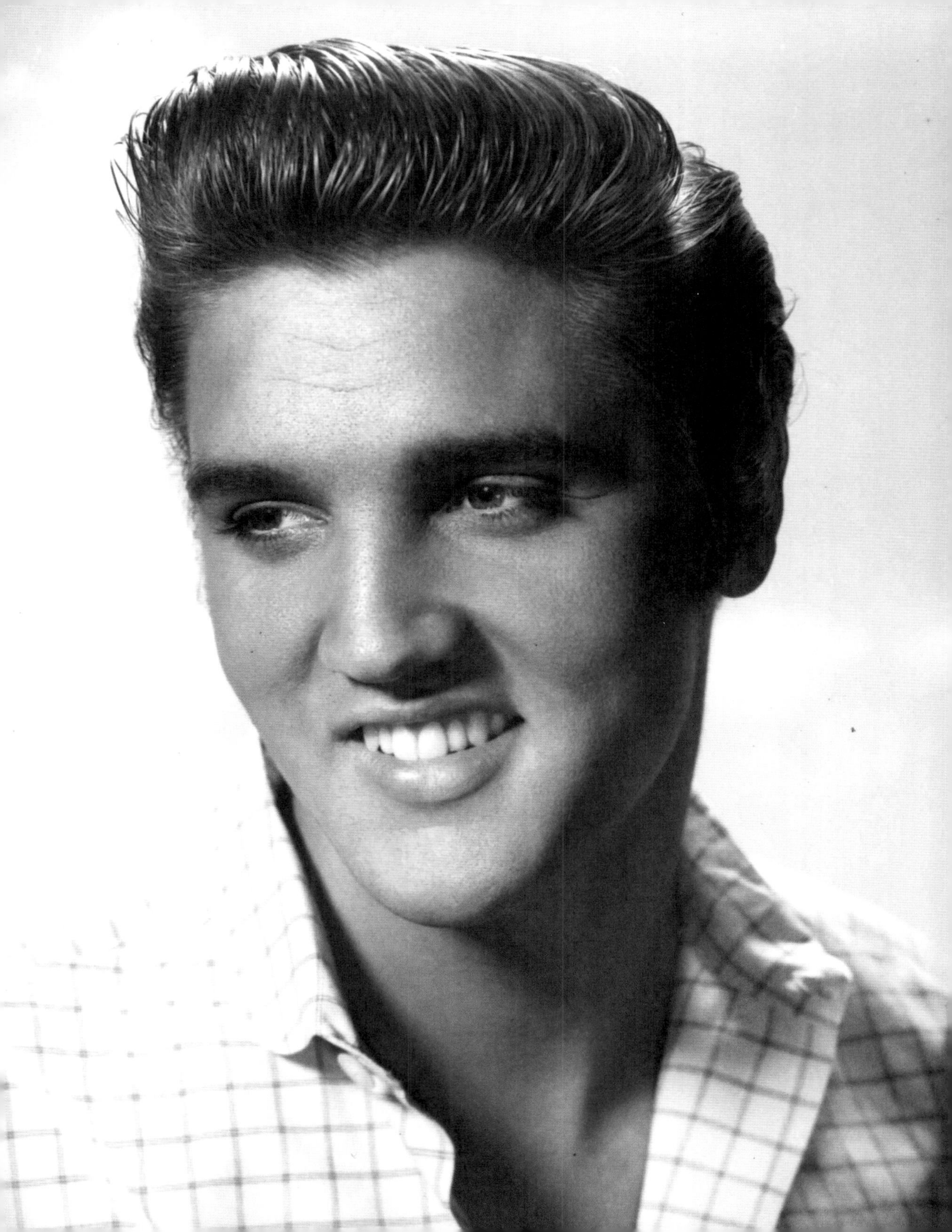

On the set of Blue Hawaii *at Paramount Pictures in Los Angeles, California, 1961*

Elvis later described the show as the most ridiculous of his career. In truth, it was a ridiculous performance. Set up by the Allen team, he was to appear wearing a bow tie, top hat, and tails singing "Hound Dog" to a basset hound on air.

Allen later wrote of Elvis that he found him "strange, gangly," and that he found his "charming eccentricity intriguing"—he was hardly enamored of the singer's style and abilities and fit Elvis into his show format for light entertainment and laughs.

Steve Allen's direct competition was Ed Sullivan. The competition between the two show hosts was well known, and Elvis benefited from their intense rivalry.

Elvis agreed to a series of three appearances on the CBS network's *Ed Sullivan Show* for a record-breaking $50,000. Sullivan put in the offer after Allen's episode that featured Elvis outdid his in the ratings.

And more record-breaking was to follow: the first appearance took 82.6 percent of the whole television audience, a figure of almost 60 million viewers. The irony was that the show was not hosted by Sullivan himself, as he was recovering from a car accident. The actor Charles Laughton instead interviewed and hosted it.

Elvis's moves and provocation were to cause intense debate and gain Sullivan even more attention. For the first two Ed Sullivan shows, Elvis was filmed from top to toe. The camera angles and filming was fairly conservative when he danced and gyrated, and yet the reaction from the audience was the same—intense screaming and near hysteria.

Elvis must have realized the impact of the show: this first appearance in September would garner him celebrity status on a never-seen-before level, millions of fans, and another record-breaking one million advance orders on his newly recorded "Love Me Tender."

But he also appeared to consider the hosts and restrictive formats of the shows with some disdain. At a concert in Memphis, he declared to the audience, "You know, those people in New York are not gonna change me none. I'm gonna show you what the real Elvis is like tonight."

Singing "Hound Dog" on The Steve Allen Show

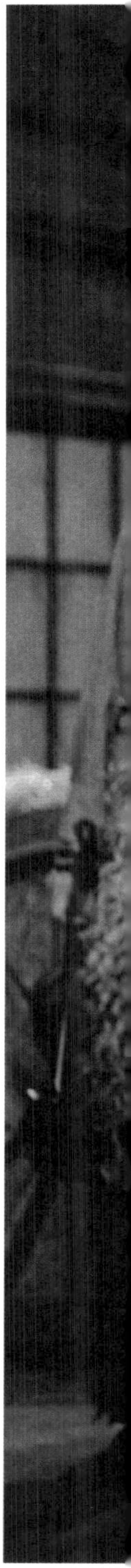

Elvis dresses up again for The Steve Allen Show

In October, his second appearance aired. In November, the film *Love Me Tender* was released, to box office success and a panning from critics. The film was originally titled *The Reno Brothers*, but Paramount cleverly changed the title to match his chart-topping single. And four musical edits were added to the acting film, taking it from a regular acted movie to the first of Elvis's famous musical films.

Following more controversy and conservative pressure, the last of Elvis's *The Ed Sullivan Show* appearances, aired in January of 1957, was famously filmed only from the waist up.

Many speculated that Parker had masterfully engineered this waist-high filming to generate even more publicity, although this remains unfounded. Regardless, Elvis still made an impact with his performance. As his hair fell seductively in his face, he provocatively mouthed the words.

In the first year of his national TV debut, Elvis made ten top singles, four of which were Number One hits. He had millions of fans and outraged just as many with his suggestive moves and raw sex appeal.

The controversy, all the talk, and the sheer number of fans meant Elvis had hit the big time. He had made it. After one year going from local star to national, in the short year that followed he had surpassed not only his own expectations, but critics', too.

Female fans push on police barricades under Studio 50 awning as they wait for Elvis to appear on The Ed Sullivan Show

Elvis performs on The Ed Sullivan Show *again, 1957*

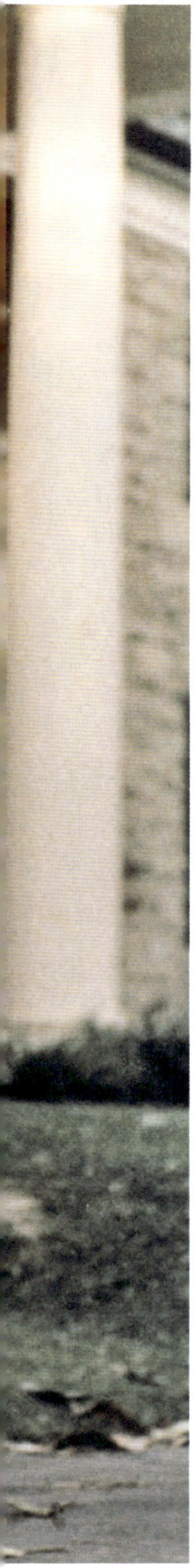

Elvis's parents remembered a young Elvis had promised them, "'When I'm grown up I'll buy you a big home and two cars. One for you and Daddy and one for me.' All his life he'd say out loud what he was going to do for us, and he'd say it in front of other people. And you know, I believed him.

"And when he got to nineteen and started making money, he told us: 'You've taken care of me for nineteen years. Now it's my turn.'"

It was following *The Ed Sullivan Show* airing in January that Elvis received notice from Memphis that it was likely he would be drafted to serve in the military later that year.

From early 1957, Elvis was already established as America's most popular act and was an international star. The singles "Too Much," "Teddy Bear," and "All Shook Up" would hit Number One on the charts. Even where his music was not officially released, Elvis was a star.

And just as Elvis had purchased a pink Cadillac car for his mother with his first advance, his first home would also be bought for his parents, as well as himself, at 1034 Audubon Drive in Memphis.

Later, he moved into a twenty-three-room Memphis mansion, Graceland, an old church that was the dream home for his family.

It was also at this time in his career that Elvis began working with songwriters Jerry Leiber and Mike Stoller. Penning "Loving You," the soundtrack to his next film, the pair helped Elvis secure his third straight Number One album.

What followed with Leiber and Stoller was a winning combination, which Elvis considered his "good luck charm." The team went on to write the majority of the tracks for *Jailhouse Rock*, of which the title track also went straight to the top of the charts as a Number One single.

Elvis Presley with songwriters Leiber and Stoller, 1957

Elvis Presley strolls the grounds of his Graceland estate in circa 1957

Elvis Presley and others dance in a scene from the film Jailhouse Rock, *1957*

Elvis while stationed in Germany in 1958

Elvis in Fort Chaffee, Arkansas, at the beginning of his military service, 1958

The *Elvis' Christmas Album* was also written by Leiber and Stoller and became the best-selling Christmas album of all time.

On December 20, Elvis's military draft notice came through. He requested a sixty-day deferment to finish the film *King Creole* (a dramatic film based on the novel *A Stone for Danny Fisher*) and, during filming, the single "Don't" (also a Leiber and Stoller special) was released, which gave Elvis his tenth Number One.

The year of 1957 closed with Elvis landing more top 100 songs than any other artist (according to Billboard).

It was time for Elvis to serve in the Army.

With his parents, family members, and some friends, Elvis reported to the Memphis Draft Board on March 24, 1958, where he and other recruits were transported to the Kennedy Veterans Memorial Hospital. Elvis's army serial number was 53 310 761. After swearing in, he was bussed to Arkansas where he and the other recruits were given the GI haircut. Stationed in Texas, Elvis was then assigned to the 2nd Armored Division's "Hell on Wheels" unit.

"Hair today, gone tomorrow."

—*Elvis coins the phrase, in a quote to the media following his drafting*

Elvis's reporting for duty was, now like the rest of his life, as far from ordinary as you could get. It was like a media "circus," with hundreds of reporters and photographers circling him as he arrived. Some photographers even accompanied him to the base, where he was sworn in.

In opposition to the amusing comment on his hair, Elvis also appeared to have a desire to be taken seriously and declared, "The Army can do anything it wants with me." He did not wish to be treated specially or any differently from other soldiers.

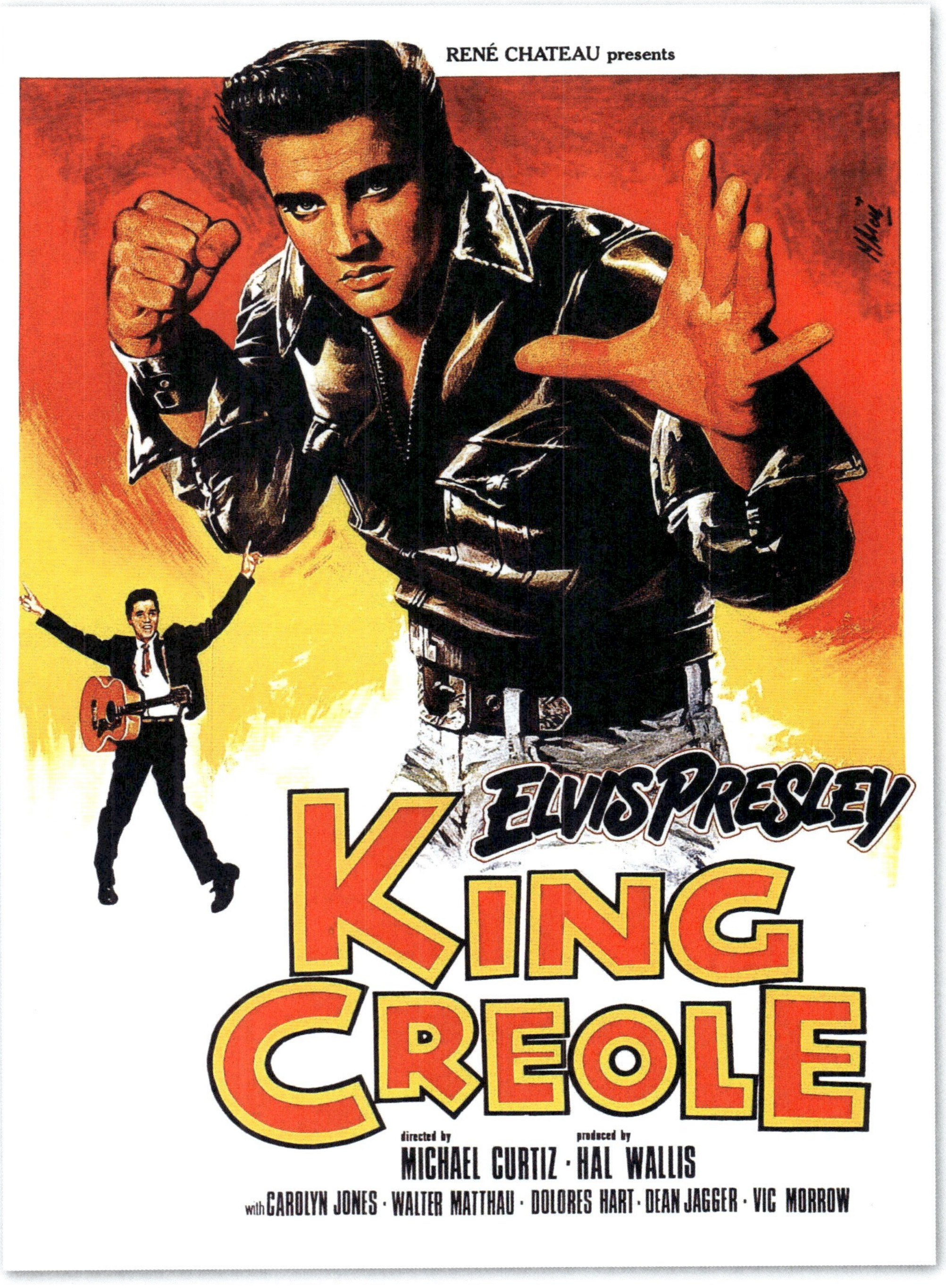

Film poster for King Creole*, 1958*

However, Presley was different. And even while he was stationed in Texas for training, he had a visit from a businessman called Eddie Fadal, who he had met on tour. According to Fadal, he was so concerned with keeping his career alive during his Army service that during a two-week leave in early June, Elvis cut five sides in Nashville.

While Elvis was in training, his mother was diagnosed with hepatitis and Elvis was approved emergency leave to visit her on August 12. Sadly, just two days later, she passed away, aged forty-six, of heart failure.

He would later name her death the greatest tragedy of his life. At her funeral, Elvis said, "You know how much I lived my whole life just for you," which showed the impact his mother had on his life and how intensely close they were. Some say he never recovered from her passing.

Following his training in Texas, Elvis was assigned to the 3rd Armored Division and was stationed in West Germany.

The Army also had a big impact on his life, some of which would be very positive and some of which was less so. He made friends in the Army and took it seriously, which was reinforced by soldiers' accounts that said he was generous and determined to be considered a good solider, just like a normal man. He donated his Army pay to charities and bought televisions for the base. He studied and practiced karate from his training.

Whether the timing of his mother's death prompted or influenced some of his choices during this period is unknown, but seems likely. Elvis was introduced to amphetamines while on duty, by a sergeant. The effect the drugs had on his energy, strength, and weight loss impressed him, and he encouraged others to try them, too. Unfortunately, this introduction would have grave consequences on his health and lifestyle later in his life.

Elvis Presley stands in line with other enlisted men and officers on a military base, Germany

Elvis with his parents while on leave from service in Germany

ESLE
SPEARHEA

Around six months later, Elvis was promoted to sergeant. He was discharged that March.

While Elvis had concerns for his career during his army tenure, he was well protected by Parker's plans and management while he was on duty. Some reported that Parker even encouraged Elvis to serve to gain respect, and that this would also be best as a soldier rather than in serving the Special Services. It was rumored Elvis was offered the Air Force, where he would have been able to perform and keep in touch with the general public. Parker was clever, though; he continued to release singles while Elvis was away, even securing a total number of ten hits in his absence. They included two Number One singles:

- **"Wear My Ring Around Your Neck" (Number Two, 1958)**
- **"Doncha' Think It's Time" (Number 15, 1958)**
- **"Hard Headed Woman" (Number One, 1958)**
- **"Don't Ask Me Why" (Number 25, 1958)**
- **"One Night" (Number Four, 1958)**
- **"I Got Stung" (Number Eight, 1958)**
- **"(Now and Then There's) A Fool Such as I" (Number Two, 1959)**
- **"I Need Your Love Tonight" (Number Four, 1959)**
- **"A Big Hunk o' Love" (Number One, 1959)**
- **"My Wish Came True" (Number 12, 1959)**

Incredibly, especially for the time, while serving in the Army, in just one year—1958—Presley earned more than $2 million.

In addition to the support and clever planning of Parker, RCA producer Steve Sholes also prepared for his Army absence by releasing a steady stream of new, unheard materials. They also compiled four albums over the two-year period and packaged it *Elvis's Golden Records*, climbing to Number Three on the LP chart.

Elvis Presley shows his sergeant insignia on February 14, 1960 in Friedberg, Germany

Left–right; Colonel Tom Parker, Eddy Arnold, and Steve Sholes at the RCA Recording studios for his last recording session for two years, on March 10, 1958

Private Presley

Elvis as lover and friend, husband and father—from accounts of his only wife Priscilla, the women he romanced, close friends, and family

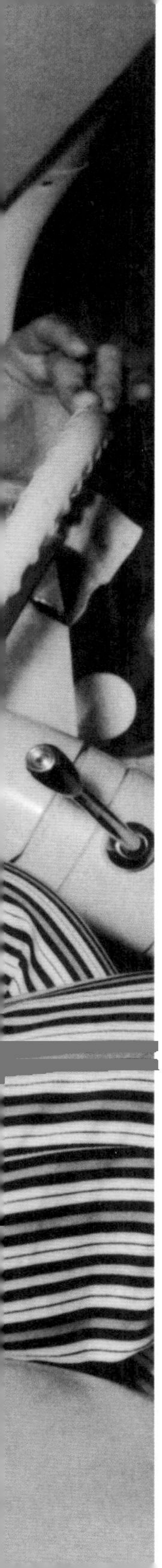

Much has been said of Elvis Presley's love life. The media and public fascination with his sex appeal and attractiveness made it inevitable. Much of it, however, is yet to be substantiated.

While Elvis was on the road to becoming a star, he had a relationship with June Juanico, and it was said of her that she was the only woman of whom Elvis's mother really approved. Whether or not this is true is unknown. Juanico wrote a book about Elvis, titled *Elvis in the Twilight of Memory* and in it she claimed they did not consummate their relationship, mainly because she was scared of falling pregnant. She also claimed that his manager, Parker, encouraged Elvis to date and be seen with beautiful women for publicity.

Of the women who dated Elvis, some have said he enjoyed an active love life, while others claim he would not pursue sex with them. Anne Helm, an actress Elvis dated, said he "really liked sex. And it was special."

This differs from his relationship with actress June Wilkinson, who he met on the set of *King Creole*, saying, "He invited me to dinner at the Beverly Wilshire Hotel . . . Then Elvis gave me a tour of his suite, sat me on the bed in his bedroom, and sang to me for two hours. That was it. The next day . . . we had dinner again. He was very sweet, and he was friendly. He had more than sex on his mind. He got me to the airport on time, and our paths never crossed again."

It was during Elvis's military service that he met Priscilla Beaulieu, a pretty fourteen-year-old brunette.

After a seven-and-a-half-year courtship, they married in Las Vegas on May 1, 1967.

Fifteen-year-old Priscilla stands amid a group of fans as she says goodbye to her boyfriend, Elvis Presley

Elvis dating a young woman in 1956, before he met Priscilla

Priscilla Beaulieu was born Priscilla Ann Wagner in Brooklyn, New York in 1945. After her father, a pilot, was killed in a plane crash when she was a child, her mother and Paul Beaulieu raised Priscilla. Captain Beaulieu was a United States Air Force Officer, who married her mother and raised Priscilla as his own.

The Beaulieus were stationed in West Germany at the same time as Elvis in his Army duty. While in Germany as a regular fourteen-year-old, Priscilla would "hang out" at the Eagles Club, listening to the jukebox, just like any other teenager. One day, a man named Currie Grant who claimed to be friends with Elvis approached her. He offered her the chance to meet him.

In a television interview with Larry King many years after Elvis's death, at Graceland, Priscilla said of meeting Elvis:

"I met him when I was fourteen. I was in Germany and he was stationed in Germany. And I was invited to go visit with him. I was actually, I was at the Eagles Club, which was a place that military families had gone to, you know, eat lunch, you know, have entertainment. And I was writing home letters to all my friends, missing them very much. And there was a guy and his wife that were there. And he introduced himself and asked me, you know, what I was doing there, how long I had been there.

"I had just—oh, my goodness, it was only three weeks that I—I had just gotten there. He asked me if I wanted to visit Elvis and did I like him. And I said yes. And I'm saying this very quickly to get it over with. I said I have to, you know, ask my parents, never, ever thinking that, you know, I would meet him."

Elvis and Priscilla drive past fans

Priscilla, now sixteen, waits with others to greet Elvis at the end of his Army tour of duty

Elvis and Priscilla in the 1960s

In September of 1959, she joined Grant and his wife at Elvis's house.

In Priscilla Presley's interview with Sandra Shevey of *Ladies Home Journal* in August 1973, not long after their divorce, Priscilla Presley talked about her romance, marriage, and divorce with Elvis.

She said of their first meeting, "It was a very casual evening—a family atmosphere. Elvis was sitting in a chair when I arrived and he got up and shook my hand. Then reality hit me, and I thought, 'What am I doing here?' Priscilla recalls that her parents were waiting up when she got home. 'They asked me how it was, and I told them exactly what had happened: that Elvis was very nice and warm and cordial, but that I never thought I'd see him again. Then he called."

"At first, my parents said that I shouldn't date Elvis, that I was too young, which was true. My mother felt that it was a once-in-a-lifetime opportunity; and besides, it was not harming me. Finally she prevailed upon Dad to consent. But he set up a 12 o'clock curfew. Each date with Elvis was the same. Usually he'd have his father pick me up in a car. Elvis's mother [Gladys Presley] had died in 1958. In Germany, Vernon was dating a pretty blond named Devanda 'Dee' Elliot. Sometimes they would join us and some friends for a movie or something.

"I was never impressed with dating Elvis. Perhaps I thought that it was all a dream. Or maybe it was because Elvis was very down to earth. He made me comfortable."

Priscilla wore a navy sailor dress with patent shoes. She said of her behavior at this time, "I was so nervous, I really didn't know what to say. I was quite shy."

Apparently Elvis said of her "Oh! A baby! You're just a kid," which was understandable considering he was ten years older at twenty-four years of age.

Elvis being asked for autographs from fellow soldiers

In unauthorized biographies, some authors claimed Elvis preferred much younger women as a way of keeping young himself.

By her account, he seemed to be trying to impress her by playing her songs. Even though she was hugely excited about meeting him, she did not tell any of her classmates at school for fear they would think she was making it up.

Though conscious of her age, Elvis wanted to see her again. They spent the following six months seeing each other. Priscilla described Elvis as gentle, fun, vulnerable, and insecure. She also said "He was a father to me. He was my mentor."

Only a couple of months before her fifteenth birthday, Elvis was discharged from the Army and moved back to the US. It was rumored that he was dating Nancy Sinatra within days of his return.

Three weeks later, Elvis telephoned and told her she was the only one. From her autobiography *Elvis and Me*, over the following two years Priscilla would become used to rumors and his denying them. Hurtfully to Priscilla, he made little of their relationship at a press conference back in the States, and he began dating Anita Wood along with other actresses.

From Priscilla's account, Elvis would discuss everything with her, including his relationship with Anita Wood. Patiently waiting on the sidelines for her King for two years, she frequently questioned her role in his life but never complained.

Elvis Presley is greeted with a gift from Nancy Sinatra upon his arrival from Europe

Left–right: Actor Nick Adams, close friend Eddie Fadal, Elvis Presley, and his girlfriend Anita Wood

Elvis poses for more film promotional posters

Out of the blue, in March 1962, Elvis called Priscilla and asked her to visit in Los Angeles. Aware that her father would object, she gave Elvis the responsibility of convincing him. Elvis ended up agreeing to a list of her father's rules, including waiting until she was on summer vacation, that he buy her a first-class round-trip airfare, to send a detailed itinerary of her activities in LA, and that she be chaperoned, write to her parents daily, and stay with his friends, the couple George and Shirley Barris.

Cleverly, and somewhat sneakily, Priscilla wrote the daily letters in advance of her trip and asked Elvis's butler to post them on her behalf.

Further deception took place when they shared a suite at the Sahara Hotel and Casino. Elvis took Priscilla shopping, and advised her what to wear, how to do her makeup and even how to style her hair. Priscilla claimed he was very instructional on her appearance, telling her that he liked women with heavy makeup.

"I was definitely under a spell of what I thought was love," Priscilla said of his controlling her appearance.

She also recalled that prescription drugs were a part of his everyday life, something she saw the first time she visited him in LA. Innocently, she did not think anything of them as they were prescribed and, even later in his life, did not think he had a problem or an addiction.

He would take sleeping pills in increasing doses over the years, and then would require prescription drugs such as Dexedrine to wake up.

She returned to visit Elvis at Graceland for Christmas, and again needed to persuade her parents to allow her to travel to him. At the end of that trip, Elvis attempted to persuade her father to allow Priscilla to finish school in Memphis. He offered the finest Catholic school and his promise she would graduate. He also promised she would be chaperoned, and would live with his father, Vernon and his new wife, and not at Graceland.

Elvis Presley and his father Vernon Presley, 1958

According to Anita Wood, Elvis was seeing both Priscilla and her at the same time. She claimed that in early 1962:

"I was coming down the backstairs into the kitchen, I heard Elvis say, 'I'm having the hardest time making up my mind between the two' . . . I knew exactly what he was talking about. And I had a lot of pride . . . so I just marched my little self right down the stairs . . . And Elvis took me into the dining room and his dad was sitting at the table. And we sat down at the table and I said, 'I'm gonna make that decision for you, I heard what you said and I'm leaving.' And I remember that I started crying, it was a very difficult decision to make. I must say that was probably the most difficult decision that I've ever made in my life. I have to say that. After having dated someone like Elvis for five years, and as close as we were for this to end. And when I left, I knew there would be no going back . . . I said, 'I'm leaving,' and I called Andy, my brother, to come pick me up and we sat there and talked a little bit longer, but nobody could eat."

In October of 1962, Elvis got his way. While he was filming *Fun in Acapulco* in Hollywood, he hosted the Beaulieus and charmed them with his hospitality. Captain Beaulieu and Vernon Presley enrolled Priscilla in the all-girl Immaculate Conception Cathedral High School. Before long, Priscilla was living at Graceland, with Vernon driving her to school. She had pocket money and was soon driving herself when she got her driver's license.

Graceland circa 1970

Elvis Presley on the set of Girls! Girls! Girls!

Priscilla also said Elvis treated her with great care and respect and did not take advantage of her saying, "We cannot compare it to today. We still had morals, high standards. There was a lot of care." She went on to claim, "Any sexual temptations were against everything he was striving for, and he did not wish to betray me, the girl waiting for him at home who was preparing to be his wife." In her autobiography, she explains they would kiss and "make out" but it never went further.

According to her account, Elvis told her that they had to wait until they were married before having intercourse. He said, "I'm not saying we can't do other things. It's just the actual encounter. I want to save it."

Some biographers have dismissed Priscilla's claims, suggesting they had a sexual relationship. But, according to Priscilla, while the couple slept in the same bed together over the six years they lived together, he would not make love with her before marriage, "somewhere, he, along in his past, said that he wanted a virgin."

Priscilla said, "Fearful of not pleasing him —of destroying my image as his little girl— I resigned myself to the long wait. Instead of consummating our love in the usual way, he began teaching me other means of pleasing him. We had a strong connection, much of it sexual. The two of us created some exciting and wild times."

She even confessed in her autobiography that they took Polaroids of their fantasies and that they were quite playful with their sexual expression, although she stressed in an interview: "Nothing was harmful; nothing was done with bad intent. Nothing was done, you know, that I don't think is unusual. They were just games."

Elvis Presley and Joan O'Brien play nurse and patient in It Happened At The World's Fair

With Ann-Margret in the film Viva Las Vegas

Ann-Margret starred in many films with Elvis

With Ursula Andress in a still from the film, Fun in Acapulco

In addition to Elvis's parents confirming he had a temper, so, too, Priscilla described his jealousy and bad temper. In her book, she claimed he threatened to dismiss an employee who was too friendly to Priscilla. According to Priscilla, Elvis would throw a chair at her if she was not fond of something he sang; that he would shoot the television using his gun if the program was not to his liking. She said, "He'd just blow them off the air; that simple. And the television would be replaced like that."

Yet, Elvis's own promiscuity conflicts with this value and expectation of her monogamy and faithfulness.

Priscilla discovered a packet of love letters from Wood in the attic at Graceland. Elvis apparently said he did not make love to Wood the whole five years he was with her. "Just to a point," he said, "then I stopped. It was difficult for her, too, but that's just how I feel."

Priscilla also understood that Elvis had affairs with costars of his films, even while he was in love with Wood.

Even though Priscilla had the company of Elvis's family, the maids, and secretaries, she reported being lonely when he was away.

While Elvis filmed *Viva Las Vegas* reports came in that Elvis and the female star, actress Ann-Margret, had started a relationship. Priscilla heard the rumors, which continued long after the movie production was finished. The chemistry between the two stars was obvious, both on and off-screen. During filming, she would try to telephone Elvis, and every time he would delay the call.

Priscilla was devastated. Because of the publicity surrounding the affair, Priscilla went to join Elvis in the following weeks while he filmed for his next movie. What followed was surprising—a jealous Ann-Margret announced to the press that she and Elvis were engaged. Unsurprisingly, the story went national.

Ann-Margret with Elvis Presley in a publicity still for Viva Las Vegas

Elvis ended up asking Priscilla to return to Memphis until the press coverage died down. Losing her temper at this, Priscilla threw a vase at the wall and Elvis starting packing her bags, telling his father to book a plane back to Germany.

In the end, on his return to Graceland, he confessed to the affair and promised it was over.

Ann-Margret was the only costar of Elvis's to attend his funeral. After his death, she wrote her memoirs and referred to Elvis as her soulmate.

Just before Christmas in 1966, Elvis went down on bended knee and proposed to Priscilla, with a three-and-a-half carat diamond ring, circled by 20 smaller detachable diamonds.

Elvis's manager, Parker, made the wedding arrangements while Elvis was off filming *Clambake*. A Supreme Court Justice presided over the nuptials, at the Aladdin Hotel in Las Vegas, in a small suite on the second floor.

Priscilla wore a white organza gown trimmed in pearls with lace sleeves and a full train. On her head, she wore a crown made of rhinestones and a three-quarter-length tulle veil. Elvis wore a black brocade suit. Fourteen guests attended the wedding, including Dee and Vernon and Priscilla's parents, the Beaulieus.

Ever the opportunist, Parker had booked a press conference immediately after the ceremony, and some of the press was even invited to the breakfast reception for one hundred guests that followed.

With their honeymoon a mere few days long—in their Palm Springs, California home—Elvis carried his new bride across the threshold singing *The Hawaiian Wedding Song*, then carried her straight to the bedroom. The newlyweds then returned to Memphis to host a reception in Graceland for family, friends, and staff. Apparently even a few lucky fans were in attendance.

Priscilla and Elvis went to their ranch near Horn Lake, Mississippi for another few days of privacy. Just as fast as the wedding itself, it was only two months later that Elvis announced on set at his latest film *Speedway* that Priscilla was pregnant.

Elvis Presley and Priscilla Beaulieu at their wedding, 1967

Priscilla and Elvis Presley at their wedding, cutting the cake

A select number were invited to the wedding

Not having been married long before her falling pregnant, Priscilla said she considered an abortion. Not because they did not want children, but because of the timing and her fear that he may find her unattractive. In her book, she said Elvis had remarked on "women using pregnancy as an excuse to let themselves go."

Priscilla controlled her weight while pregnant, dieting to the extent that she weighed less at full term than prior to the pregnancy. She reported the couple had an active love life during her pregnancy. And then the rumors came about Elvis and his costar of the film *Speedway*, Nancy Sinatra.

Elvis reassured her that the rumors were untrue, saying she must have been sensitive because of her pregnancy. While six months pregnant, Priscilla received a telephone call out of the blue from Nancy Sinatra, who was Frank Sinatra's daughter, offering to throw her a baby shower. Elvis convinced her to accept, even though Priscilla found it peculiar coming from a woman she hardly knew. However, she and Sinatra got along well.

Shortly after the baby shower, Elvis asked Priscilla for a separation, saying he was confused. Days later, he changed his mind.

On February 1, 1968, their only child, Lisa Marie, was born.

In an interview with Sidney Fields, Elvis's parents talked about his nature, how he'd been brought up and his values.

"He's never sassed us and he's never been uppity. Big people are still the same as little people to him, and he's considerate of both the same way. We're country folk. He's a country boy, and always will be. How can any boy brought up like mine be indecent or vulgar? Especially when he's so good to us and his friends. Why, he always wants to do what's right," said his mother.

Elvis and Priscilla proudly show their newborn baby, four-day-old Lisa Marie

Elvis starred with Nancy Sinatra in Speedway, *1968*

His father continued, "He never touched a drop of liquor in his life, and he wouldn't know dope if he saw it.

"He's a sympathetic boy, and tender-hearted. It hurts him when someone thinks bad of him. Maybe this will tell you what he's like. He was usherin' at the movies this time, and on his night off he was downtown with his friends and he sees this Salvation Army lady takin' up the Christmas collection. But the box was empty. Elvis put his last $5 bill in it, and started drummin' up a noise to get that box filled. It was filled."

His own values and upbringing would have an impact on how he wanted to behave as a husband and father. By Priscilla's, and indeed, all accounts, Elvis was a doting father to his only daughter.

Priscilla said of his parenting, "He adored having a child. He adored Lisa. He just loved watching her grow up. He was a very caring father."

Elvis was generous to a fault with his daughter, he rarely disciplined her and allowed her almost anything she wanted.

Priscilla, on talking with Larry King about jewelery she bought Elvis, said of his generosity:

"The pendant is a gift that I gave him, actually, in 1967, I believe. It was from our favorite jeweler at the time, Harry Levitch. It's a calendar in the back marking his birthday with a ruby and diamonds on the side. You know, Elvis did like a lot of flash. He loved jewelery and he liked getting jewelery. He was more of a giver, though. He loved giving gifts more than he did receiving gifts."

Despite these extravagances, Elvis also liked regular things, such as watching old movies. His favorites included *It's a Wonderful Life* and *Wuthering Heights*.

The family at home

Elvis doted on Lisa Marie

The year of Lisa Marie's birth was also the year of Elvis's return to the limelight. From 1967 to mid-1968, his singles climbed no further up the charts than number 28. To a rock star accustomed to regular Number One hits, this was devastating. To overcome this, his manager Parker began to focus again on Elvis's television appearances to raise his profile and popularity, organizing a Christmas special that aired in December of 1968.

It became known as the '68 Comeback Special and viewers tuned in to watch in record numbers. He had found renewed fame and success, which was positive for the marriage, but also meant regular touring and time away from his young family.

After the success of his comeback, Elvis again filmed away from his family, for an MGM production titled *Elvis on Tour*. It went on to win a Golden Globe for Best Documentary Film. While his success returned, and with it his career fulfillment and happiness, Elvis's family life was becoming just the opposite.

In 1971, Elvis had an affair with Joyce Bova, who had become pregnant and aborted the baby. He was unaware of this at the time, but it signaled his lack of discretion and care for his immediate family and reputation. In addition to the absences from home, Priscilla thought Elvis was no longer interested in her sexually, that he could not see her the same way after she became a mother.

She grew lonelier. Elvis was taking pills to fall asleep and Priscilla found more letters from girls in their Palm Springs home. After Elvis asked her not join him on tour as much, her paranoia and sadness about his promiscuity worsened. She also had two affairs of her own, and just four years later their marriage was over. Priscilla claimed that after her confession to an affair with Mike Stone, her karate instructor, Elvis forced himself on her and said, "This is how a real man makes love to a woman."

Priscilla Presley poses for a portrait holding her little poodle circa *1965*

Tom Jones poses with Elvis Presley and his wife Priscilla, Las Vegas, Nevada, July 1, 1971

They separated. In just five months time, Elvis had moved his new girlfriend, songwriter and ex-beauty queen Linda Thompson, into Graceland. Thompson was reportedly a virgin and she said they did not consummate their relationship until they had dated for a few months. Thompson was a fan of gospel music and shared Elvis's curiosity for spiritual and religious enlightenment.

It was claimed that their earlier passionate relationship eventually became depressing and dispassionate. Thompson said of Elvis, "There were times when he was very, very, difficult. There was a lot of heartache and he exhibited a lot of self-destructive behavior, which was very difficult for me, you know, watching someone I loved so much destroy himself."

Elvis Presley and his wife Priscilla leave the courthouse hand in hand following a short divorce hearing on October 9, 1973

Elvis and Priscilla filed for divorce in August of that same year. When the couple divorced, Priscilla recalled "The judge couldn't believe it." They remained very close even after their divorce.

According to Elvis's friends, however, he was not happy about the divorce and worried about his age and his career. According to many, Elvis never got over the failed marriage.

Sadly, before his death, Priscilla joked with Elvis that maybe it might be their time again, together. Elvis joked, "I'm seventy and you're sixty. We'll both be so old, we'll look really silly, racing around in golf carts."

"Elvis epitomized charm, charisma. But I think his laughter. Elvis had the most contagious laughter. He just—once he started laughing, that was it. Everyone would start laughing. And sometimes it was uncontrollable. He couldn't stop.

"And he laughed over the silliest things, you know?

"He just—he just had a great sense of humor. He loved to have fun. He loved to play games."

—Priscilla Presley, on what she missed most about Elvis after he died

A family portrait from 1970

The King is Back

On return from military service, Elvis was keen to regain his career status as The King

When Elvis returned to television after his Army service, it was only a short two months later and it would be for an unheard of amount of money. Parker had booked Elvis for just eight minutes of singing time, for $125,000. Titled the "Welcome Home Elvis" episode for a television program hosted by Frank Sinatra, who must have overcome his disdain for rock 'n' roll.

Elvis was also desperate to regain his status at the top of the charts. The pressure to deliver was massive and he was already being asked what his immediate plans were now that he was a regular citizen again. It was two years since he had been in a recording studio and at the press conference on his return, he seemed not to know what the process would be, "As far as when I'll record, I really don't know," he said. "Probably this week or next week. And what I'll record, I don't know yet. I've got quite a few songs to choose from, I've collected over two years. I don't know exactly what type or what instruments I'll use . . . I really don't know yet."

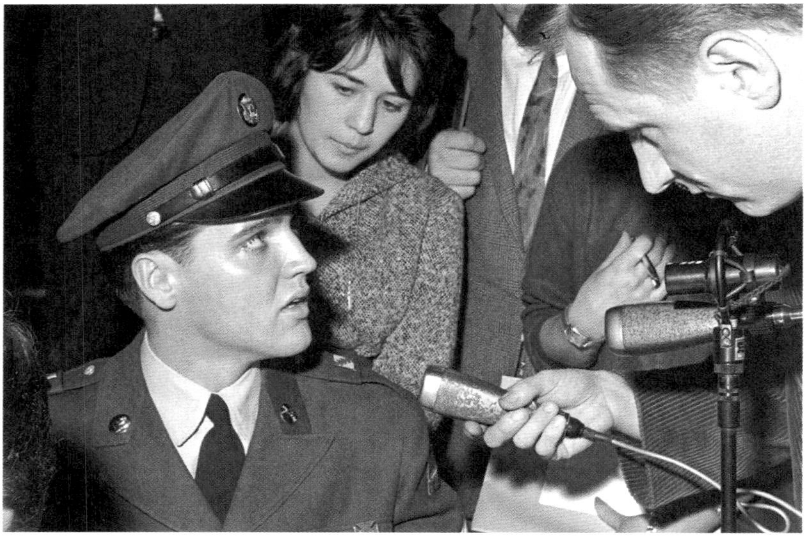

Elvis at a press conference following his return from the army

"Well, the first thing I have to do is to cut some records."

—Elvis at Press Conference at Graceland, March 7, 1960

Elvis gets back into the swing of things, 1960

But Parker and RCA knew exactly what was planned for the session in two weeks time. One session in Nashville, then a break while Elvis filmed the Sinatra television special, then back in the studio to record new material.

Parker allegedly brought "Are You Lonesome Tonight?" into the studio to be recorded by Elvis, as a request of his wife, it being one of her favorites.

RCA had organized an A-list group of musicians to record with Elvis for his return, including Hank Garland on guitar, Bob Moore on bass, Buddy Harman on drums, Floyd Cramer on piano, Boots Randolph on saxophone, and the Jordanaires on vocals. Elvis insisted his old band members Scotty Moore and D.J. also be included. Using new technology, as Ernest Jorgensen explained in his book on Presley's recording sessions, "This would be the first time Elvis was recorded on a three-track machine, giving more space to each player (as well as a separate track for Elvis's voice) and making real stereo records possible. For a group of sophisticated players like this, three-track was a distinct advantage: The music they made could be reproduced in finer detail."

Floyd Cramer was drafted in on keys

Boots Randolph, a new recruit to Elvis's band

Elvis gets back into the studio

The first session was an eleven-hour recording, the second one almost twelve hours long. According to engineer Bill Porter, there was serious tension in the control booth from where the RCA management team watched. They needn't have been concerned.

As the biographer Peter Guralnick declared, "There was nothing on the session that could not be said to be of a very high standard." Some declare it his best artistic and commercial work in his career. There were eighteen songs in total:

- **"Make Me Know It"**
- **"Soldier Boy"**
- **"Stuck on You"**
- **"Fame and Fortune"**
- **"A Mess of Blues"**
- **"It Feels So Right"**
- **"Fever"**
- **"Like a Baby"**
- **"It's Now or Never"**
- **"The Girl of My Best Friend"**
- **"Dirty, Dirty Feeling"**
- **"Thrill of Your Love"**
- **"I Gotta Know"**
- **"Such a Night"**
- **"Are You Lonesome Tonight?"**
- **"The Girl Next Door Went A'Walking"**
- **"I Will Be Home Again"**
- **"Reconsider Baby"**

Jorgensen said, "Elvis had never been heard like this before . . . There was new depth to his voice; his interpretations were increasingly sophisticated; the group was probably the best studio band in the business; the song selection was imaginative and varied, the technical quality excellent . . ."

The Jordanaires remained as backup singers

Elvis looking thoughtful in a promotional shot from the 1960s

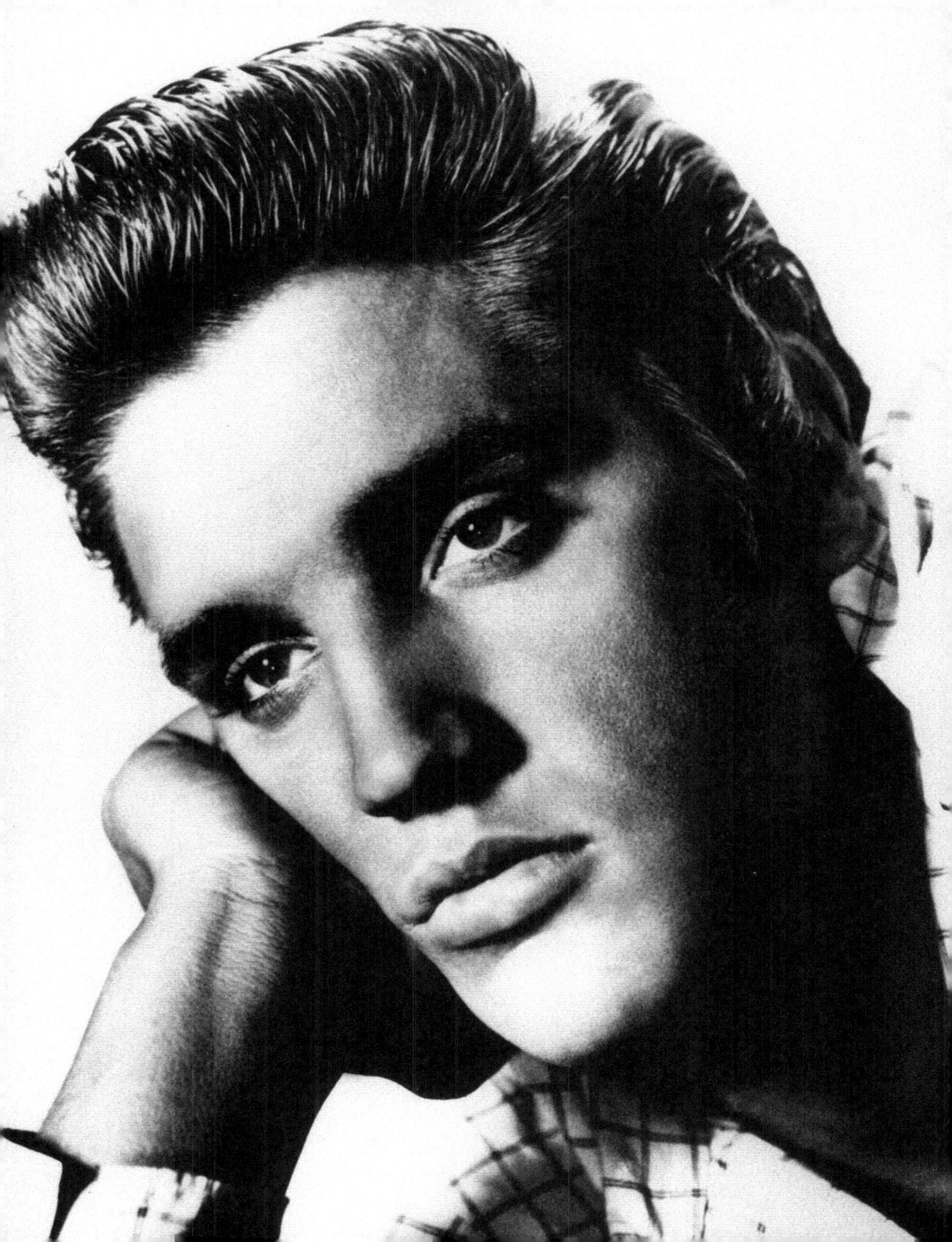

"Most surprisingly of all, the new album didn't point in one particular musical direction . . . It was as if Elvis had invented his own brand of music, broken down the barriers of genre and prejudice to express everything he heard in all the kinds of music he loved.

"As a document of Elvis's first comeback, *Elvis Is Back* was irresistible."

"Stuck on You" had four weeks at Number One on Billboard's "Hot 100" pop chart. Then "It's Now or Never" spent five weeks at Number One, and "Are You Lonesome Tonight?" followed with six more weeks at Number One. The album itself was his first to be released in true stereo, and it reached Number Two on the charts. The RIAA labeled it a Gold Album in 1999.

The RCA executives and Parker were pleased. Elvis's fans were still buying his records and when the previously critical (of rock 'n' roll) Frank Sinatra said, "Presley has no training at all. He has a natural, animalistic talent. When he goes into something serious, a bigger kind of singing, we'll find out if he is a singer," Elvis looked set to prove he was.

Inspired by Elvis's admiration for Tony Martin's "There's No Tomorrow," the single "It's Now or Never" was quite different from Elvis's earlier sound. The same could be said of "Are You Lonesome Tonight." The diversity of singles featured on the album, along with the diversity of his vocals, would cause some critics to rethink their prior judgments of Elvis.

Elvis, Nancy Sinatra, and Frank Sinatra

Elvis smiles for the camera, 1960

Elvis Presley rehearsing for his appearance on The Ed Sullivan Show, *October 1961*

Elvis poses with a new acoustic guitar

For example, "It Feels So Right" was rock 'n' roll rebellion and "The Thrill of Your Love" was gospel-inspired. The album also covered blues, with Elvis on rhythm guitar throughout the tracks.

With superb warmth and depth, this stereo album sounded great and looked great. It featured full color photographs of Elvis, taken just before he was discharged from the Army.

More critically acclaimed than any of his other albums recorded across his career, it continues to be praised and was awarded four-and-a-half stars by *Rolling Stone Magazine* in 2011, saying "Elvis is Back! Might be the King's greatest non-compilation LP: wildly varied material, revelatory singing, impeccable stereo sound."

Many have commented on his return and surmised that while he was on duty with the Army, Elvis must have worked hard on his voice range and quality, building its strength and power for his return. Of the tape cut and left off the released album, it was said the rejected recordings were not too removed from the quality of those included. With a high quality band and Elvis's more mature, rich vocals, these unreleased edits could easily have been used.

Elvis Presley plays drums in a moment off camera while filming the movie Flaming Star, *1960*

Elvis was self-critical and apparently apologized before taping "Fever," saying, "If I hit a few bad notes here because I can't get my bearings right, you know, but uh, we got plenty of tape."

Both the artist and the band were keen to reach near perfection. In some takes, there would be adjustments to musical arrangement or tempo in order to reach the pinnacle of musical excellence. With a full, long day in the studio for both recordings, there was no doubt Elvis and his band worked exceptionally hard to deliver the commercial success and critically acclaimed quality of *Elvis is Back*.

Following his success with the album release and his television debut, there was one last medium Elvis needed to conquer on his return from service: cinema.

Slated by the critics, his first film on return from the Army, *G.I. Blues* was fluffy and unimaginative, like many of his movies. However, Elvis's soundtrack to his first film on his return from service, *G.I. Blues*, went to Number One in October and the film itself did well at the box office. Elvis's movie career was a disappointment to him in many ways, despite the commercial success.

Elvis in costume for G.I. Blues

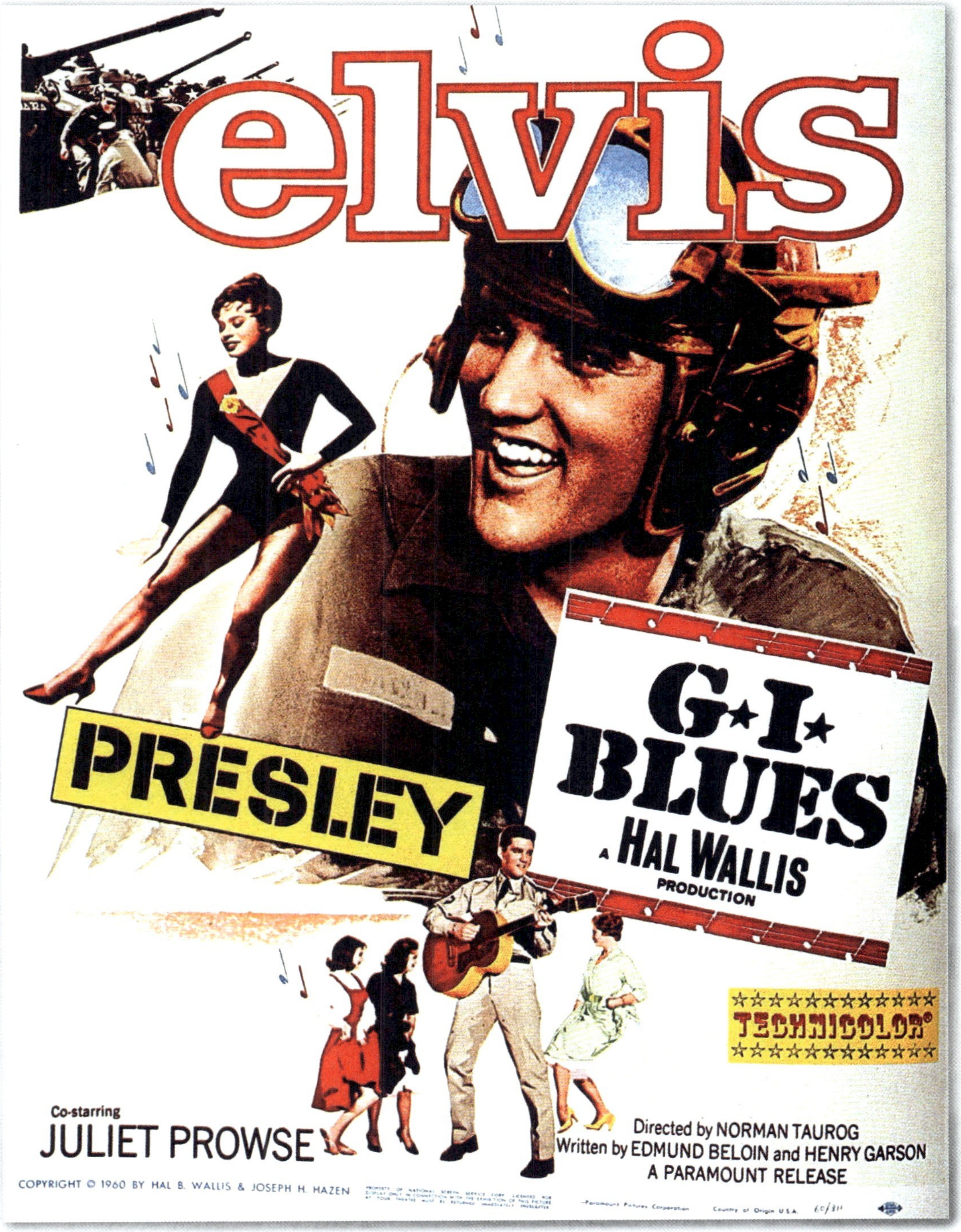

Film poster for G.I. Blues

Elvis Presley, surrounded by babies, in G.I. Blues *1960, his first movie after leaving the Army*

The Music and the Moves

Famous for his lopsided grin, sideburns, greased hair, and husky voice, Elvis added to his appeal with some outrageous moves for his time

"Some people tap their feet, some people snap their fingers, and some people sway back and forth. I just sorta do 'em all together, I guess."

—Elvis Presley in 1956

His moves began to find their exaggerated form around the time he hit the big time in 1957, and became a key part of his act throughout the 60s. And the mere presence of The King, let alone his famous pelvic moves, sent the audiences into a tizzy. Elvis's long-time support band member, Moore, remembered the live performances around this time:

"He'd start out, 'You ain't nothin' but a Hound Dog,' and they'd just go to pieces. They'd always react the same way. There'd be a riot every time."

"Rock and roll music—if you like it, if you feel it, you can't help but move to it. That's what happens to me. I can't help it."

—Elvis Presley

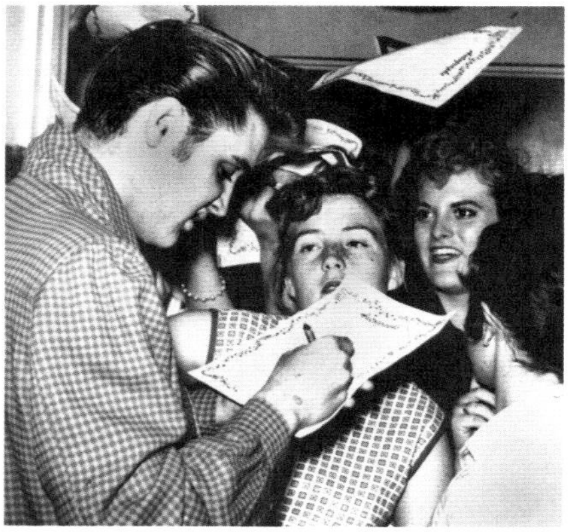

Signing autographs for adoring fans

A screaming crowd of teenage girls has to be restrained

GRAHAM

In fact, even at this early point in his national popularity, there were security concerns surrounding his performances. Fifty national guardsmen were stationed at the concerts he performed for at the Mississippi-Alabama Fair and Dairy Show. What followed was chaos. A performance in Wisconsin prompted the local Catholic diocese to write to the director of the FBI, J Edgar Hoover, advising him,

"Presley is a definite danger to the security of the United States . . . [His] actions and motions were such as to rouse the sexual passions of teenaged youth . . . After the show, more than 1,000 teenagers tried to gang into Presley's room at the auditorium . . . Indications of the harm Presley did just in La Crosse were the two high school girls . . . whose abdomen and thigh had Presley's autograph."

His television performances seemed to worsen the visibility and controversy of his moves. It was Milton Berle who first encouraged Elvis to go on without his guitar and Elvis obliged with a raunchy, slow version of "Hound Dog" and matched it with raunchy, slow grinding movements of his hips.

The audience rush the stage at the Mississippi Dairy Show

Elvis performs onstage with his brand new Martin D-28 acoustic guitar at Fort Homer Hesterly Armory 1955

Elvis plays "Hound Dog" to adoring fans

Elvis grabs the microphone during a performance, 1955

Critics berated him with dismissive comments regarding his voice and focused on his hip swiveling, with reviews such as Ben Gross' of the *New York Daily News* ". . . Elvis, who rotates his pelvis . . . gave an exhibition that was suggestive and vulgar, tinged with the kind of animalism that should be confined to dives and bordellos".

Even Ed Sullivan, prior to inviting him to his show with that record-breaking amount, apparently informed his producers, on reviewing the Berle show tapes, that Elvis's moves were inappropriate for Sunday viewing for families.

But Elvis's least favorite was the term "Elvis the Pelvis," spurring him on to say that it was a childish comment to come from a grown man.

The controversy surrounding his moves and his live act continued. In August of 1957, Elvis was ordered by a judge from Jacksonville, Florida to tame his movements.

From accounts of the performance that followed, Elvis kept his body still, and teased both the audience and the order by wiggling his little finger suggestively.

"The first time that I appeared on stage, it scared me to death. I really didn't know what all the yelling was about. I didn't realize that my body was moving. It's a natural thing to me. So to the manager backstage I said, 'What'd I do? What'd I do?' And he said "Whatever it is, go back and do it again."

—From a 1972 taped interview used in MGM's documentary Elvis on Tour

"I'm not trying to be sexy. It's just my way of expressing myself when I move around."

—Elvis Presley

Elvis's second appearance on The Ed Sullivan Show

Backstage at The Milton Berle Show

Elvis continued to tour during the year of 1957, to riots, crazed fans, fainting, and crying girls.

In Vancouver, the crowd destroyed the stage at the end of the act and a riot broke out. In Philadelphia, he was pelted with eggs. In Detroit, the local newspaper warned: "the trouble with going to see Elvis Presley is that you're liable to get killed."

Later, in the words of his obituary for Elvis, Lester Bangs credited him as "the man who brought overt blatant vulgar sexual frenzy to the popular arts in America."

His physical and sexual appeal was undeniable. That his moves promoted this is also undeniable. But his now grown-into, handsome, dark good looks were on their own, striking. Even the male critics of his time were expressive of the fact. Mark Feeney said, "He was once beautiful, astonishingly beautiful".

Television director Steve Binder said, "I'm straight as an arrow and I got to tell you, you stop, whether you're male or female, to look at him. He was that good looking. And if you never knew he was a superstar, it wouldn't make any difference; if he'd walked in the room, you'd know somebody special was in your presence."

Elvis poses seductively for a promotional shot

Possessed with this natural sex appeal and blatantly employing raunchy pelvic movements during his live performances, Elvis captured the eye and the imagination of women and men, teenagers, and critics across the world. But his sound, voice, and musical genre were just as appealing and intriguing.

For many music fans, even today, Elvis Presley introduced them to rhythm and blues. The link from his blues roots to his pioneering rock 'n' roll is obvious when listening to many of his songs. Starting with his first recording of "That's All Right," Elvis's sound was the white man singing the blues. Elvis often altered the song lyrics of rhythm and blues numbers he covered, to make room for his fast tempo rockabilly style.

Elvis's musical roots in country, gospel, and rhythm and blues were obvious, but he always returned to gospel, inspired by its uplifting and moving style. His attendances at the All Night Singings at the Ellis Auditorium in Memphis would give him style influence for his sound—as well as his moves.

Elvis Presley (left) and Liberace exchange personal trademarks while standing together.

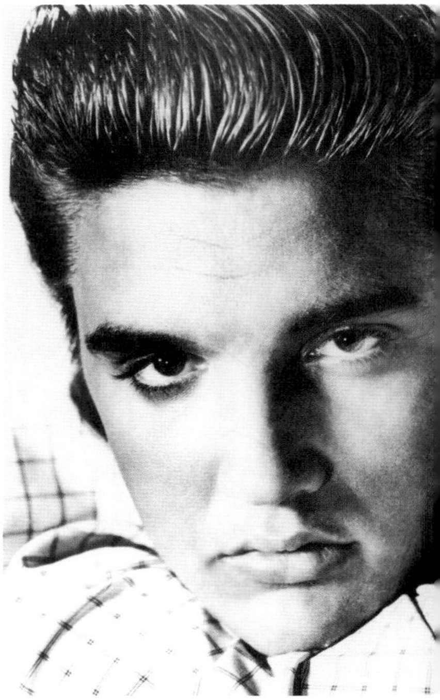

Another seductive pose to promote his upcoming films

Posing with a brand-new twelve-string guitar

Acts like the Statesmen Quartet featured highly emotional vocals. Ironically, it was at church and at these gospel nights that Elvis first witnessed the power of the jiggle, where the leader of the Quartet employed a sprinkling of leg jiggling.

His musical influences continued to be wide-ranging, and like any music fan, he had a comprehensive knowledge of his favorite genres. Leiber and Stoller reported how impressed they were by his understanding of the blues. And equally, his knowledge of gospel was impressive. Even Elvis himself announced to the press: "I know practically every religious song that's ever been written."

In late 1957, Elvis dropped by Sun Records studios. Phillips was no longer Elvis's sponsor or manager. That day he captured a recording of an impromptu session. Elvis was jamming with Carl Perkins and Jerry Lee Lewis, which resulted in the Million Dollar Quartet (although the fourth member of the recording, Johnny Cash, was only there briefly and reports were he did not record with the other three).

Left–right; Jerry Lee Lewis, Carl Perkins, Elvis Presley (sitting), Johnny Cash—The Million Dollar Quartet

Elvis Presley and Johnny Cash pose for a portrait in December of 1957

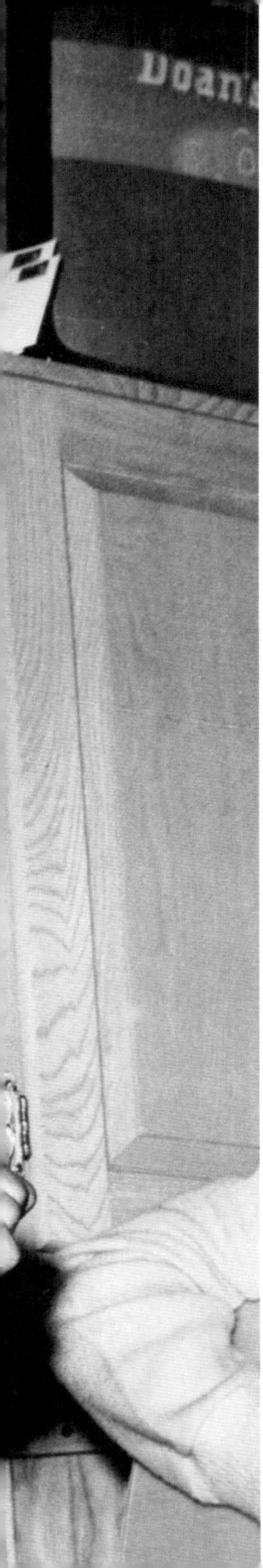

Elvis's sound grew from his love of gospel, fused with country and blues, into his own distinct sound heightened with a raw, emotive, rhythmic twist. Once he'd moved from Sun to RCA, he continued to grow his sound and his moves—blending electric guitar to further the rockabilly style with a tougher edge.

Interestingly, on his return from military service, Elvis pushed his sound into another realm, with what was then described as a more mild rock beat. This lighter sound flowed into the soundtracks of his post-Army filmography.

Considering his meteoric rise to success, it must have been important to Elvis to return to civilian life with musical and film success. Not even a month out of his Army fatigues, Elvis went back to the recording studio to work on his first stereo album *Stuck on You* and met up with Frank Sinatra to tape the television program *The Frank Sinatra-Timex Special*. This was interesting, considering Sinatra had previously been highly vocal and critical of the rock 'n' roll genre.

Some accounts of Sinatra's criticism claim it was directly about Elvis, the following presented quite regularly in stories: "His kind of music is deplorable, a rancid smelling aphrodisiac. It fosters almost totally negative and destructive reactions in young people."

Elvis Presley plays a double-necked electric guitar, 1966

Whether this was actually said by Sinatra, of Elvis, is yet to be proved and it seems questionable.

The following, however, is a direct quote from an article in the *Los Angeles Mirror News* (October 28, 1957):

"My only deep sorrow is the unrelenting insistence of recording and motion picture companies upon purveying the most brutal, ugly, degenerate, vicious form of expression it has been my displeasure to hear—naturally I refer to the bulk of rock 'n' roll.

"It fosters almost totally negative and destructive reactions in young people. It smells phony and false. It is sung, played and written for the most part by cretinous goons and by means of its almost imbecilic reiterations and sly, lewd—in plain fact, dirty—lyrics, and as I said before, it manages to be the martial music of every sideburned delinquent on the face of the earth … this rancid-smelling aphrodisiac I deplore. But, in spite of it, the contribution of American music to the world could be said to have one of the healthiest effects of all our contributions."

Frank Sinatra

Elvis poses for a portrait in 1960

That same day, Elvis was apparently asked his reaction to Sinatra's comments about rock 'n' roll. From reports in several LA newspapers the following day, there were various versions of his response presented. The one most attributed is from the *Herald-Express*, by Gerry McCarthy, who quoted Elvis as saying:

"He has a right to his opinion, but I can't see him knocking it for no good reason. I admire him as a performer and an actor but I think he's badly mistaken about this. If I remember correctly, he was also part of a trend. I don't see how he can call the youth of today immoral and delinquent. It's the greatest music ever and it will continue to be so. I like it, and I'm sure many other persons feel the same way."

This conversation is a fascinating insight into the debate that raged at the height of Elvis's success. Right from a young age, Elvis divided opinions: his peers, his teachers, and talent scouts. Some found his looks, his style, and his voice too different, too unusual. The majority, however, ended up determining him a cultural and musical icon, a revolutionary.

Elvis and Frank Sinatra joke together in 1965

Elvis performs on a small stage to the adulation of a young crowd, 1957

Elvis recording with the Jordanaires

Ballads such as "Are You Lonesome Tonight?" also went to Number One. It seemed that whatever musical journey Elvis took his fans on, they loved. His later career also went through various permutations, from the strong, almost aggressive rock sound of his 1968 *Comeback Special*, to his later soul and funk infused recordings of the tracks on *Suspicious Minds*.

Elvis's last recordings in the 70s had a country sound and were often played on local country radio stations, taking him back to where he came from, musically and as a star.

In addition to Elvis's much-talked about musical style, his voice has had a variety of reviews and commentary and has been declared both a baritone and a tenor. His range was brilliant, with some describing it as two octaves and a third, others stating it was two and a quarter octaves. His vocal capacity for high Gs and As is similar to those an operatic baritone would possess.

Elvis during his Comeback Special, *1968*

Gibson

An intimate shot taken during Elvis's 1968 Comeback Special

Much has been written of his vocal style, in an emotional sense (surely steeped in his gospel musical upbringing). Lindsay Waters, music scholar, states: "His voice had an emotional range from tender whispers to sighs down to shouts, grunts, grumbles, and sheer gruffness that could move the listener from calmness and surrender, to fear. His voice can not be measured in octaves, but in decibels; even that misses the problem of how to measure delicate whispers that are hardly audible at all."

In this way, it is difficult to compare Elvis's style, voice, and vocal ability or range to anyone else.

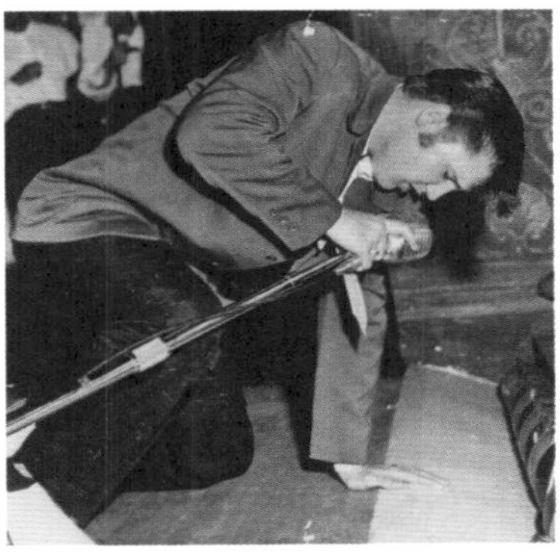

Elvis's distinctive vocal sound combined whispers, grunts, and sighs

"A live concert to me is exciting because of all the electricity that is generated in the crowd and onstage. It's my favorite part of the business—live concerts."

*—Elvis at a press conference prior to his 1973 television special, called "Elvis—*Aloha from Hawaii, via Satellite"

Hollywood and the Movies

Elvis was keen to be considered a genuine and talented actor

He looked up to James Dean and Marlon Brando and dreamed of being a movie star. Despite Elvis's natural success with music, he knew he would have to learn a lot and work hard to become an actor.

Starting out in film, Elvis said in an interview with the press, "I've talked to veteran actors. I've talked to a lot of producers and directors in Hollywood, and they all give you advice … they told me that I had good possibilities.

"I think I'm gonna enjoy it. I really do."

Elvis's phenomenal roll call of films is thirty-three-long.

While many fans are aware of his work with Hollywood producer Hal Wallis, from Paramount Pictures, he actually only appeared in nine films out of thirty-three in total for Wallis. The majority of his films were for Metro-Goldwyn-Mayer.

Beginning with 1957's *Jailhouse Rock* to the last 1969 film, *The Trouble with Girls* in 1969, Elvis starred in 12 films for MGM. The studio also produced Presley's documentary films in the 1970s.

His first few films are generally viewed to be the better ones of his career, perhaps because he was involved in choosing the options.

Elvis's very first film was a nerve-wracking experience for the team of filmmakers and, presumably, for Elvis himself. Indeed, the transference of singer and rock star to movie actor was and continues to be challenging. It was set for release in 1956 and those behind it were undecided as to whether Elvis would prove a success on the big screen. He had participated in three days of screen tests in March for Wallis at Paramount in Hollywood and it took a week for Wallis to offer a contract. The contract was signed in April, for one film with an option for six more.

"I have never read a line. I never studied acting, never been in any plays or anything—I just got out there."

—Elvis on acting, in an interview in 1956

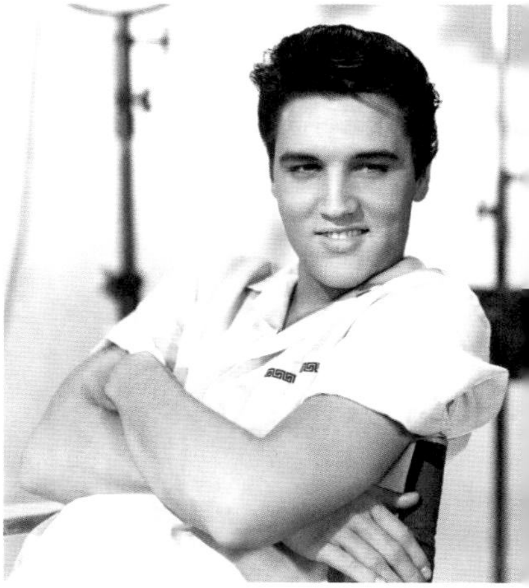

Elvis relaxing on set circa 1960

Elvis alongside Judy Tyler in Jailhouse Rock

Originally titled *The Reno Brothers*, at the time of signing, Elvis was still a rising star and had not received national attention—that all changed when he appeared on the Milton Berle and Steve Allen shows that summer. With all the fuss and fan worship that soon followed, they included four songs and adapted it from a straight acting film into a musical retitled *Love Me Tender*.

Interestingly, it has been reported that the final scene in the movie had two possible outcomes—for the main character played by Elvis to live or to come to a violent death as described in the original script. After much debate, including a vote between the 20th Century Fox board of directors, they reached a compromise with Elvis's character dying to save the life of his screen brother, followed by a shot of him walking up in Heaven singing the theme song.

Even more interestingly, the filmhouse gave theaters the choice of two endings: the final edits being one version with his character appearing in a shadowed form as his family walks away from the grave and the second version ending on his death. The surveys that came back showed most theaters went for the softer version so as not to incite upset in filmgoers and fans of Elvis.

While much talk and reservation came with Elvis's launching a film career, he actually won over the film crew and his fellow cast. His costar Richard Egan praised Elvis to the press, saying, "This guy is genuine. There's nothing phony about him and he works hard. He's not conceited. He IS self-assured, but that's fine with me. I'm all for him and all of us associated with him in the picture are rooting for him." (from an interview with Charles Gruenberg of *The New York Post*)

A publicity handout for Love Me Tender

Elvis Presley kisses Debra Paget in a still from Love Me Tender

Presley dances in front of his band in a movie still from 1957

He went on to say to Sheilah Graham's *Hollywood Today* review, "Elvis is a surprising type of actor. He's the male Monroe. He's completely without guile. You give him lines and he says them the way he would in real life. And that's the best kind of acting—when you're not."

The film was launched and screened on Broadway at the Paramount Theater in New York on November 15, 1956.

Unsurprisingly, considering Parker's tendency to maximize Elvis's appearances when there was an offering to promote, he had booked the singer for a series of public appearances coinciding with the opening of the film.

The film opened at the Paramount in Toledo just a day before his stage show played the city's Sports Arena on Thanksgiving Day. As it turned out, both his show and the film did very well in ticket sales. Parker would later choose to starve audiences of Elvis in person whenever one of his films was released. It was, in fact, why audiences continued to watch his films: to see The King on screen.

Following the key learnings from Elvis's film debut, Wallis understood that a Broadway premiere was not necessary—as long as the films were released where teenage fans lived, there would be great ticket sales.

He also knew the fans were there to see Elvis and to see him sing, not necessarily to watch him act. As long as Elvis was the star, on the promotional posters and in the full feature length of the film, the sales would continue to come in.

Elvis poses for a portrait in 1956

This formula was employed for Elvis's next movie, *Loving You*, where Elvis sang only six minutes into the movie. Generally considered his best, the next three Elvis movies were more serious. According to reports, he had pushed for more serious roles in the early 60s, including *Flaming Star* and *Wild in the Country*. They did not do as well at the box office.

Playing a bad boy rock 'n' roll rebel in *Jailhouse Rock*, Elvis received positive critical feedback on his acting. It premiered in Memphis on October 17, 1957, and was released nationwide on November 8.

It continues to be a much loved film of his, and in 2004 the US National Film Registry selected it for preservation for being "culturally, historically, or aesthetically significant."

King Creole proved to be a rare example of how a serious acting role could be combined with Elvis singing on screen. However, even when it was obvious that such a combination wouldn't work in every film, Parker continued to pressure the studios to include music. In his fourth movie, Elvis gave the best performance of his film career, portraying an angry and confused young man.

"As the lad himself might say, cut my legs off and call me Shorty! Elvis Presley can act. It's a pleasure to find him up to a little more than Bourbon Street shoutin' and wigglin'. Acting is his assignment in this shrewdly upholstered showcase, and he does it, so help us over a picket fence."
—Howard Thompson of the New York Times

On return from military service, Parker had Elvis booked on a tight film schedule. The films were mostly predictable, small budget musicals. Each turned a profit.

Tuesday Weld and Elvis Presley in Wild In The Country

Elvis Presley stands shirtless in a scene from the film Flaming Star, *1960*

A Hollywood movie producer once said: "A Presley picture is the only sure thing in Hollywood." Another sure thing was high sales of the soundtracks. There was a formula for these, too. Leiber said it was "three ballads, one medium-tempo [number], one up-tempo, and one break blues boogie." But with Elvis averaging three films a year, the timing was tight not only on filming, but on song writing and production.

The Jordanaires' Gordon Stoker said of the soundtracks, "The material was so bad that he felt like he couldn't sing it."

Again, regardless of critics' attacks on the music material, from 1960 to 1964, three of his soundtrack albums reached Number One.

Under the management of Parker, however, and certainly while Elvis was away on duty for the Army, he had less and less of a say in which roles were his. This meant the serious, more credible roles went by the wayside. Nevertheless, the films were always a success in ticket sales, if not in critics' reviews.

Parker had the ultimate control while Elvis served in the Army. He worked with the Hollywood studios to set up an approach, an "Elvis formula" that would generate high ticket sales and repeat success.

Parker was a fantastic negotiator. He strategically bumped Elvis's salary up by playing the studios off one another and demanding higher salaries for each new contract. A good example of this was the first movie Elvis was to star in after returning to civilian life. In contrast with the $15,000 agreed for his first film with Wallis at Paramount in 1956, Parker negotiated an incredible fee of $175,000 for *G.I. Blues* in 1958. Plus, he negotiated a cut of the movie's profits.

Parker did not interfere, however, with the script, production, or indeed any aspect of the filmmaking process. He encouraged Elvis to do the same and accept orders.

Talking to a Fox executive for Elvis's first film, Parker said, "There's no sense in sending me the script. The only thing I'm interested in is how much you're gonna pay me."

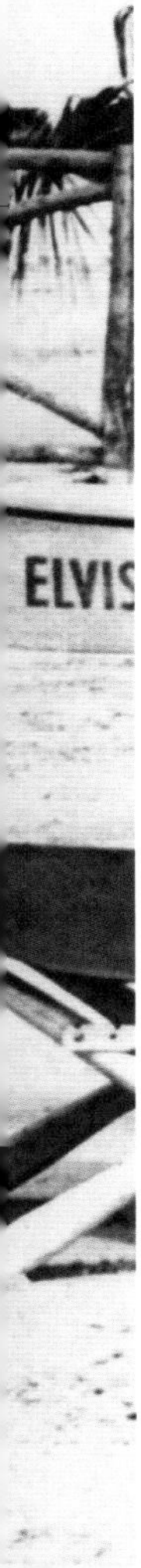

Elvis Presley with manager Colonel Tom Parker—holding a gun to him, early 1960s

The Colonel continued to release films while Elvis served in the Army

"We don't have approval on scripts—only money. Anyway what's Elvis need? A couple of songs, a little story and some nice people with him. We start telling people what to do and they blame us if the picture doesn't go. As it is, we both take bows and if it doesn't hit maybe they get more blame than us. Anyway, what do I know about production?—nothing."

—Colonel Parker in an interview with Variety *magazine*

The only element Parker pushed for in Elvis's films was the music. He knew that the fans wanted to see Elvis sing and that would mean commercial success. One report of the 1960 film *Flaming Star* came back with the story of the director David Weisbart having stated, "I cannot see how it is possible for Elvis to break into song without destroying a very good script."

Allegedly, Parker responded "We want all the best possible results for this picture, including the hundreds of thousands of dollars worth of exploitation represented by a good record release by Elvis."

After testing with audiences, however, on this occasion the director won, with only the title tune and one other song appearing in *Flaming Star*.

"This isn't a very popular view, but Colonel's formula was correct. The serious stuff—the movies that didn't have many songs in them—flopped. That's a pretty good argument. On the other hand, by the time Elvis figured out he was being screwed around, it was too late. He signed too many contracts. If the Colonel handed him a contract, he'd sign it and never look at it … And when you've already been paid for the pictures, and you've already spent half the money, you've got to do them. All those pictures were presigned. So Elvis had no choice."

—Lamar Fike, Elvis's friend and confidante

Elvis Presley in Flaming Star, *1960*

Elvis behind the scenes at M.G.M.

M·G·M

Elvis Presley plays ukelele in Blue Hawaii, *1961*

Elvis poses for a promotional photo in 1960

A musical comedy, his first after his return from the Army, *G.I. Blues* was slated by critics. It was, however, to become the template of Elvis's future movie formulas.

Made in 1960, it was lightweight and only finished fourteenth on *Variety's* list of the year's top grossing films. Just one month later, they released *Flaming Star*, a western drama largely considered his best acting of the three westerns he starred in. *Star* came in much lower in box office sales, a point attributed to the fact that the movie does not feature any Elvis songs. The audiences told the movie producers through these sales what they wanted to see: Elvis singing.

Elvis admitted as much in an interview with *Parade* magazine in 1962:

"I'm smart enough to realize that you can't bite off more than you can chew in this racket. You can't go beyond your limitations . . . A certain type of audience likes me. I entertain them with what I'm doing. I'd be a fool to tamper with that kind of success. It's ridiculous to take it on my own and say I'm going to appeal to a different type of audience, because I might not. Then if I goof, I'm all washed up, because they don't give you many chances in this business."

Elvis's seventh film was titled *Wild in the Country*, in which both his acting and script were criticized for being "sheer nonsense" by the *New York Times* reviewer Bosley Crowther.

Blue Hawaii, released with fourteen songs and filmed with beautiful South Seas scenery, made up for the previous poor reception to *Wild in the Country*. The music and the comedic script gave it the winning formula to make it Elvis's most successful film of his career.

Elvis's last day serving in the Army

Elvis wears an Army uniform for his role as Tulsa McLean in the 1960 film G.I. Blues

The soundtrack album to *Blue Hawaii* became the most successful LP of Elvis Presley's career. It went straight to the top of Billboard's album chart and stayed at the Number One position for an incredible twenty weeks.

The film led to sales of the soundtrack LP, and the album led to repeat ticket-buyers for the film. In the plot, Elvis plays a very likeable, energetic adult tour guide to a group of teenage girls. Famously, Angela Lansbury plays the funny girl role as Elvis's mother.

More light story lines followed with his films *Follow That Dream, Kid Galahad, Girls! Girls! Girls!, It Happened at the World's Fair*, and *Fun in Acapulco*. The roles Elvis played in these films varied from prizefighter and fisherman to playboy pilot.

In *Fun in Acapulco*, Elvis sings eleven songs, and as his character is a lifeguard who travels to Mexico, he sang some Mexican songs. His serious rock 'n' roll days were left behind to make way for light, scenic musical numbers. Released in 1963, the film came out at a time when Elvis was beginning to feel unhappy with his career.

In 1964, MGM's *Kissing Cousins* began to negatively impact Elvis's perception—as the director Don Siegel said, Elvis was "kind of a joke in the industry as an actor." In this film he sings nine songs.

Parker, being heavily involved in the money-making aspect of Elvis's film career, was beginning to insist on tighter budgets and even tighter shooting schedules. *Viva Las Vegas* pulled in $9.44 million to finish at number eleven, while *Kissin' Cousins* suffered a number twenty-six spot with $3 million.

For, despite *Viva Las Vegas* being one of 1964's top box office films, production costs ate up the predicted high profits of its release. *Viva* is one of the most exciting Elvis films to watch, mainly because of the chemistry between Elvis and Ann-Margret. It also featured great music and lots of it.

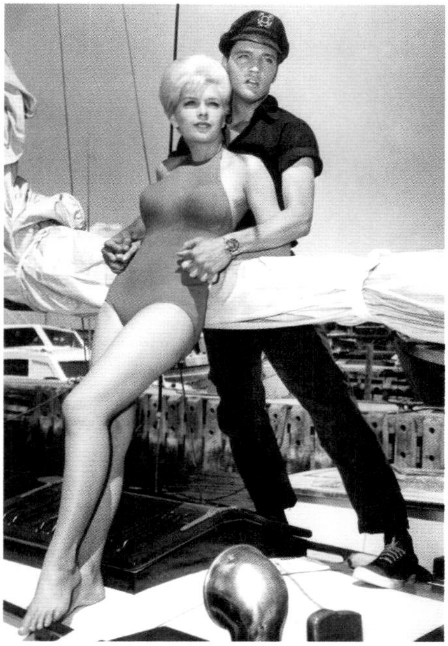

Stella Stevens and Elvis Presley on board and holding hands in a scene from the film Girls! Girls! Girls!

Elvis singing on screen in Blue Hawaii

The second half of the decade did not perform quite as well. Still, the gospel single "Crying in the Chapel" was a top ten hit and the gospel album *How Great Thou Art* was to win Elvis his very first Grammy Award for Best Sacred Performance.

After Elvis married, his career of films and accompanying soundtracks written and produced to the formula that sold tickets continued until the release of *Clambake* resulted in low sales. Audiences appeared to have had enough of the now tired Elvis formula.

His filmography that followed included *Roustabout, Girl Happy, Tickle Me, Harum Scarum, Frankie and Johnny, Paradise Hawaiian Style, Spinout, Easy Come Easy Go,* and *Double Trouble.*

Tickle Me was Elvis's first non-musical comedic role. In the majority of his other films, he chases girls, while playing a singing lead role, some more heroic than others.

Again, critics despised it, with *The New York Times* warning, "Elvis Presley had better watch his step after 'Tickle Me,' his latest color musical film. This is the silliest, feeblest, and dullest vehicle for the Memphis Wonder in a long time. And both Elvis and his sponsors, this time Allied Artists, should know better.

"In such trim packages as 'Viva Las Vegas' and 'Fun in Acapulco,' the Presley formula—colorful settings, tunes, and pretty girls aplenty—took on real, tasty sparkle. But yesterday's flapdoodle, even weaker than the preceding 'Girl Happy,' should strain the indulgence of the most ardent Presley fans. See for yourself, girls. It looks made up as it goes along."

Elvis Presley in the movie Harum Scarum

Elvis Presley in Roustabout

Marlyn Mason and Elvis Presley in The Trouble With Girls

Clambake followed, with Elvis playing a wealthy young man pretending to be a normal ski instructor. It was his first film as a single man, following his divorce. His acting was the last thing on his mind, and many have said this was his worst performance of his movie career. He had put on weight and his audiences were starting to show disinterest in his appearances on the big screen in the same way he was.

His last six films were unremarkable. *Stay Away Jose, Speedway, Live a Little Love a Little, Charro!, The Trouble with Girls*, and *Change of Habit* saw gradual declines in ticket sales.

The next three films to feature Elvis were documentaries and would prove much more successful with audiences. Following his '68 *Comeback Special*, Elvis fascination had peaked again and the live, behind-the-scenes footage of The King doing what he did best, performing, would help strengthen his status as The King of Rock 'n' Roll once again. In 1970, Elvis's performance at the International Hotel in Las Vegas was scintillatingly captured in *Elvis: That's the Way It Is* and the fifteen-city concert tour of Elvis's in 1972 recorded in the hugely popular *Elvis on Tour*.

For many, *That's the Way It Is* was a revelation, and a revolution in documentary filmmaking. Indeed, if fans did not get to see him in Vegas, they could take it all in with this film. MGM kept the focus on Elvis, with the editing featuring slices of fan commentary appearing throughout. Aside from the fan edits, the film featured a simple three-part format, in chronological order.

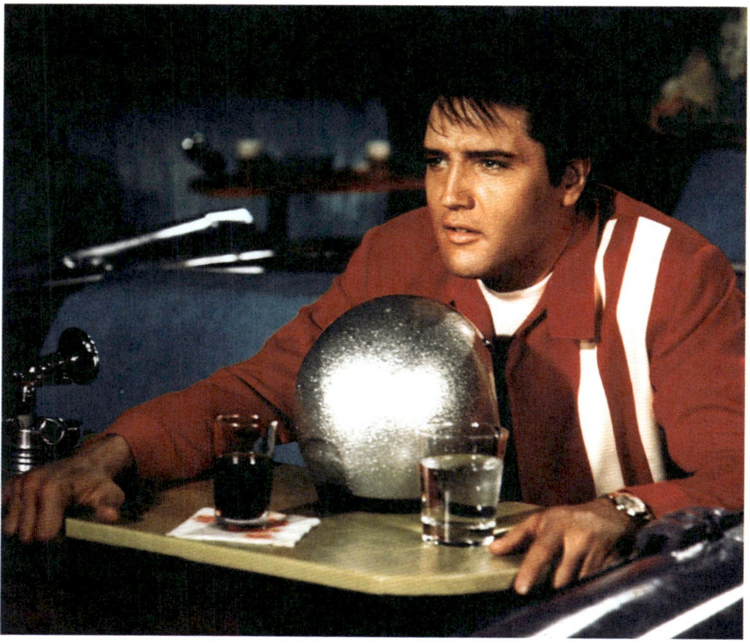

Elvis Presley in the movie Speedway

"The first 20 minutes of the film are devoted to studio rehearsals, cross cut with fast excerpts from personal interviews with fans. The rehearsal horseplay comes off very well. Then onto Vegas for about 26 minutes of pre-opening preparation by both Presley and the hotel staff. Finally, most of the remaining hour-plus comprises actual show numbers culled from several live performances."

—Variety *magazine*

The director, Denis Sanders, captured the essence of Elvis live and punctuated the film with snippets featuring fans to highlight the phenomenon that was Elvis fever. This is also evident with the inclusion of a feature on an Elvis fan convention. Elvis, who was thirty-five years old in this documentary, appears in good shape and powerful onstage.

This time, the *New York Times* review was kinder:

"The callow youth who gyrated to fame and wealth as a kind of national joke is now a handsome man, a bit jowlier, true. But the face has character. The personality is a bit more suave but stronger. The powerhouse drive that used to flail about wildly is shrewdly disciplined and siphoned until it explodes into his extraordinary sense of rhythm. Tired? Elvis? He's ferocious. Most impressively of all, he comes over as a genial, reasonably balanced guy . . . Years later, the Presley act has an actor and a good one."

The only criticism leveled at the documentary was the lack of behind the scenes Elvis, to show what kind of person he was. There are a handful of moments where the viewer catches a glimpse—when he is nervous about going onstage, for example. But there is no footage of Elvis's family, his wife and daughter, or his manager. It was a glimpse of Elvis's as a live persona more than the man off-stage.

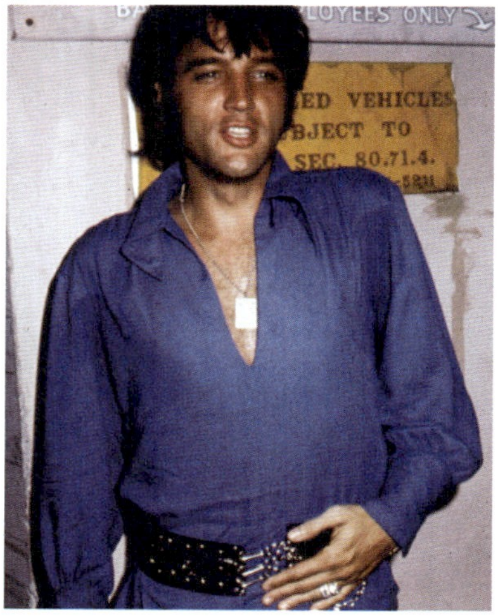

Elvis backstage during his USA tour, 1970

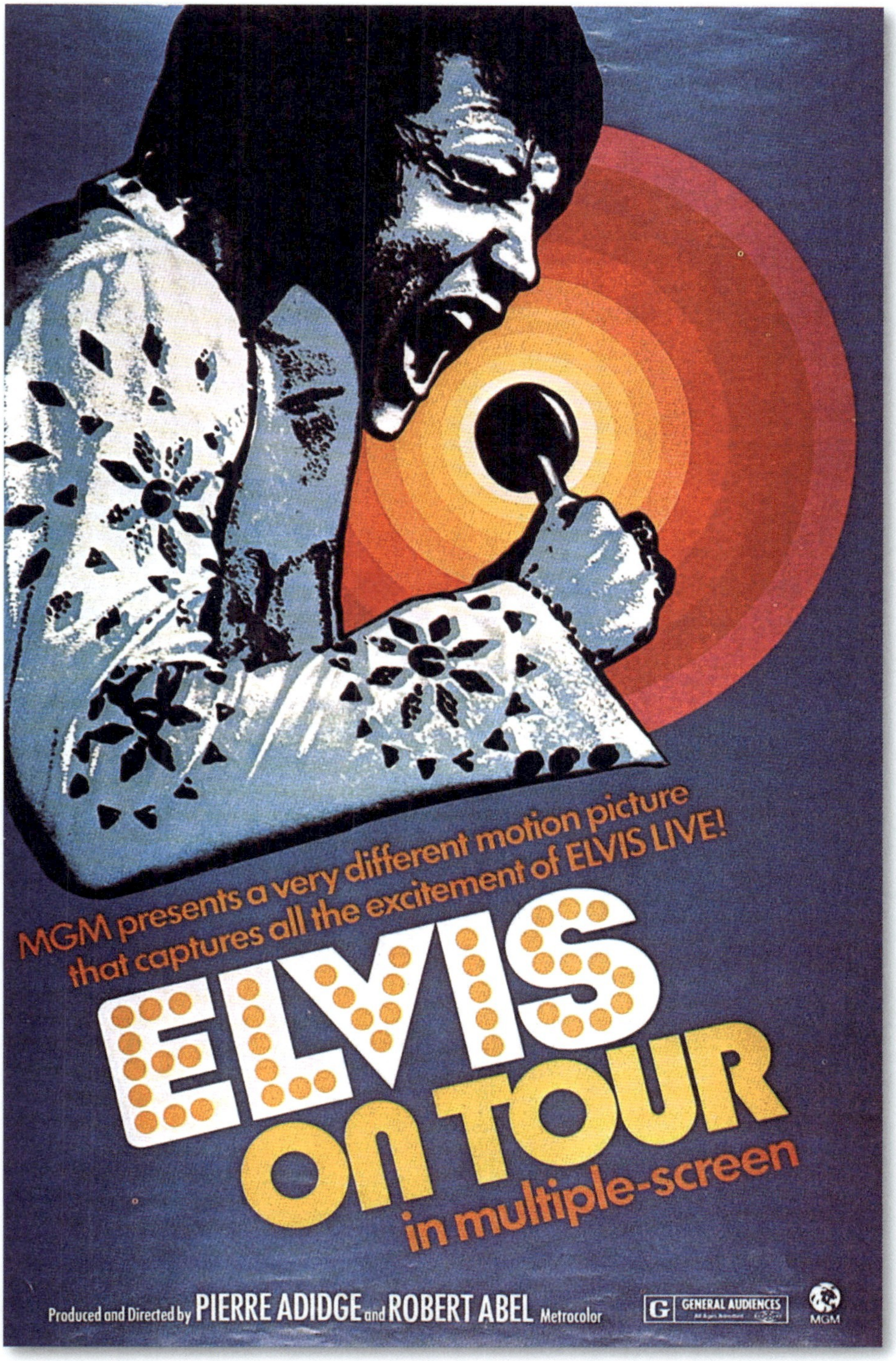

Film poster for Elvis on Tour

Elvis Presley performs onstage in 1972

Elvis wearing a white rhinestone-studded suit, 1975

The follow-up documentary *Elvis on Tour* was a more entertaining view of Elvis live, with the producers and directors Pierre Adidge and Robert Abel taking the viewer on a journey using panels, where footage was spliced on-screen. It's in this documentary that the viewer can see Elvis in jumpsuits and it signals the beginning of his final years.

"Bill Belew's wardrobe for Presley's onstage concert appearances make the star resemble Captain Marvel, which isn't far off the mark considering what Presley has accomplished in an 18-year period of worldwide fame. The musicianship is updated of course, but the adroit insertion of some old Ed Sullivan guesting footage places the early days in complementing, not contrasting context."

—Variety *magazine*

This documentary was less successful with audiences, taking around $490,000 in 105 cities over the first weekend. The *New York Times* was even less supportive of the film, with reviewer Canby opining that the film was nowhere near an intimate portrayal of the star, "The camera never catches him in a truly candid moment. Close-ups do not reveal anything but, rather, they enshrine an ideal . . . while getting on and off airplanes, on and off buses and in and out of limousines. Strip away the storybook myth and—lo—there is a storybook myth underneath; a nice, clean-cut, multi-millionaire pop idol who is, offstage, hard-working and friendly and something less than a riveting personality. The essential blandness of the offstage Elvis has the effect of diminishing the impact of what we see of the onstage performances."

Five years later, Elvis would be dead.

Elvis performs onstage in 1972 in a studded jumpsuit

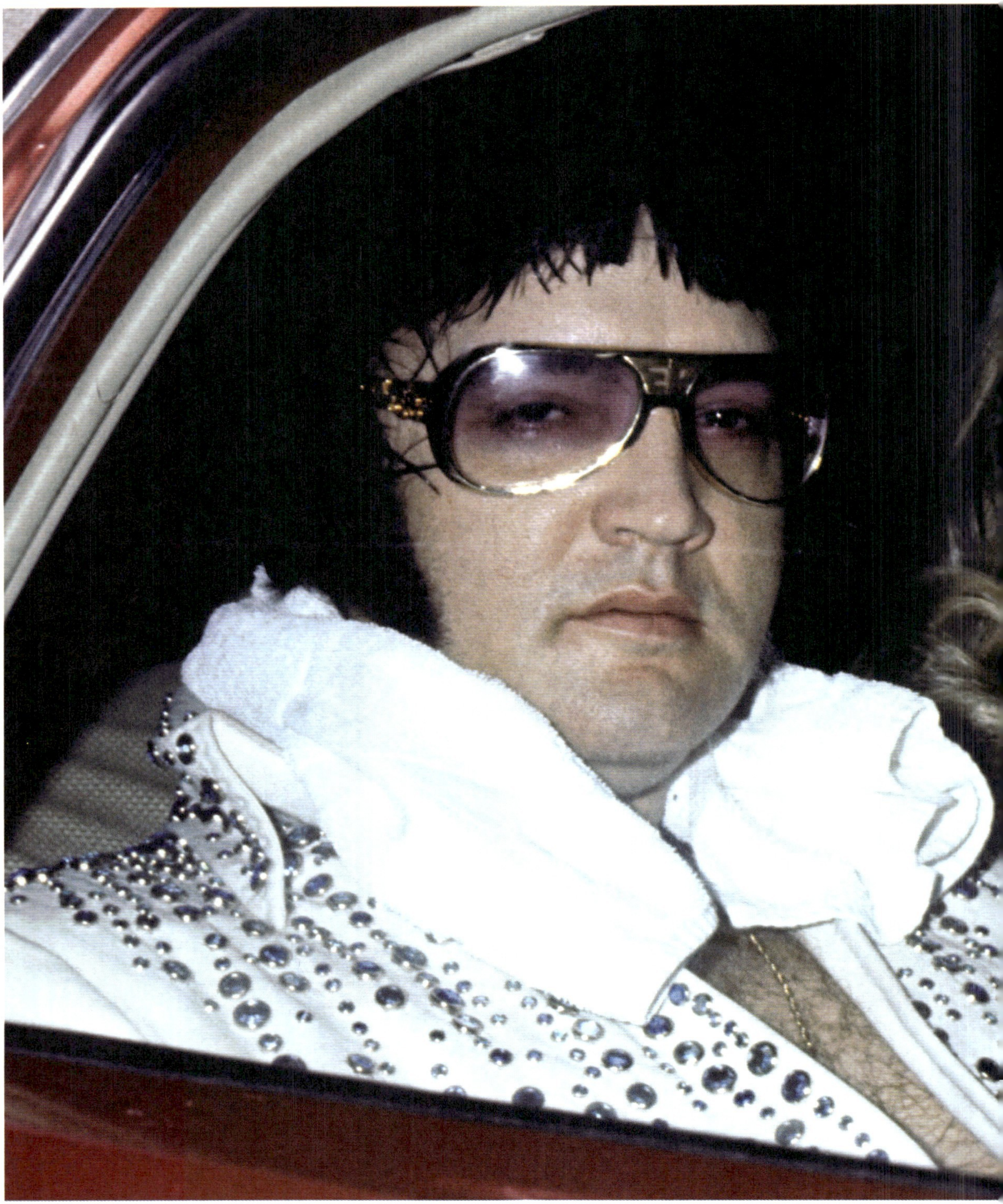

The final film to be made and released in 1981, posthumously, was considered by many fans as the best of the three documentary films, simply titled *This is Elvis*.

Named "The definitive film biography of The King" by Dave Marsh of *Rolling Stone* magazine, this is Elvis on a fascinating journey.

The documentary makers had full access to Elvis's estate and included for the first time some home movie sequences. The first version of this film featured staged versions of events, with voice stand-ins, the remastered version released a couple of years later begins with Elvis arriving at Graceland on the last night of his life.

While the film is not in chronological order, it covers the majority of Elvis's career highlights. Only the first three of his movies are covered though. There is more focus on the wedding of Elvis and Priscilla, Lisa Marie, and it shows clips of his appearances across various media, including television.

The viewer also sees some less complimentary footage, hearing Elvis's friend talk in some detail about Elvis's drug use and his peculiar behavior later in his life. The film shows Elvis in his later years, overweight and forgetful of lyrics onstage in Vegas. It is considered to be a well-put-together documentary of Elvis's life, featuring the good, the bad, and the ugly.

"So maybe we never win an Oscar—but we're going to win a few box office awards. Check the list of the 10 top box office stars—Elvis is right there. And here's a guy who carries his pictures by himself—the rest of the guys on the list have three or four stars to back them up."

—Colonel Parker

Elvis and Linda Thompson arrive at the International Hotel, Las Vegas

Elvis, Father of Lisa Marie

His only child, daughter Lisa Marie, was nine years old when he died

On learning of her pregnancy, Priscilla was devastated. Sharing her family story with British newspaper *The Guardian* in 2012, she wrote "I thought, 'Oh my gosh, here I am married and now I'm pregnant and I'm not going to look attractive any more.' It was certainly a rocky time. It was hard for Elvis too because he was a sex symbol—the most wanted sexual specimen in the world. And he was apprehensive about what his fans would think about him being a dad and how that would affect his status as a sex symbol."

According to Elvis, he said his biggest accomplishment in life was his daughter. He liked that his name would carry on after his death, and considered it incredible he had helped create Lisa Marie. It was said that she was the light of his life.

He adored Lisa Marie. He spoiled her.

The recipient of regular gifts, jewelery and toys, Lisa Marie had the life of a young princess, befitting of the daughter of The King. One story tells of his overindulgence, flying her by private jet so she could see and play in the snow. For her first birthday, he rented out the whole amusement park, called Libertyland, for Lisa Marie and her friends.

Elvis and Priscilla Presley with their daughter, Lisa Marie, 1968

The Presley family at home in Graceland

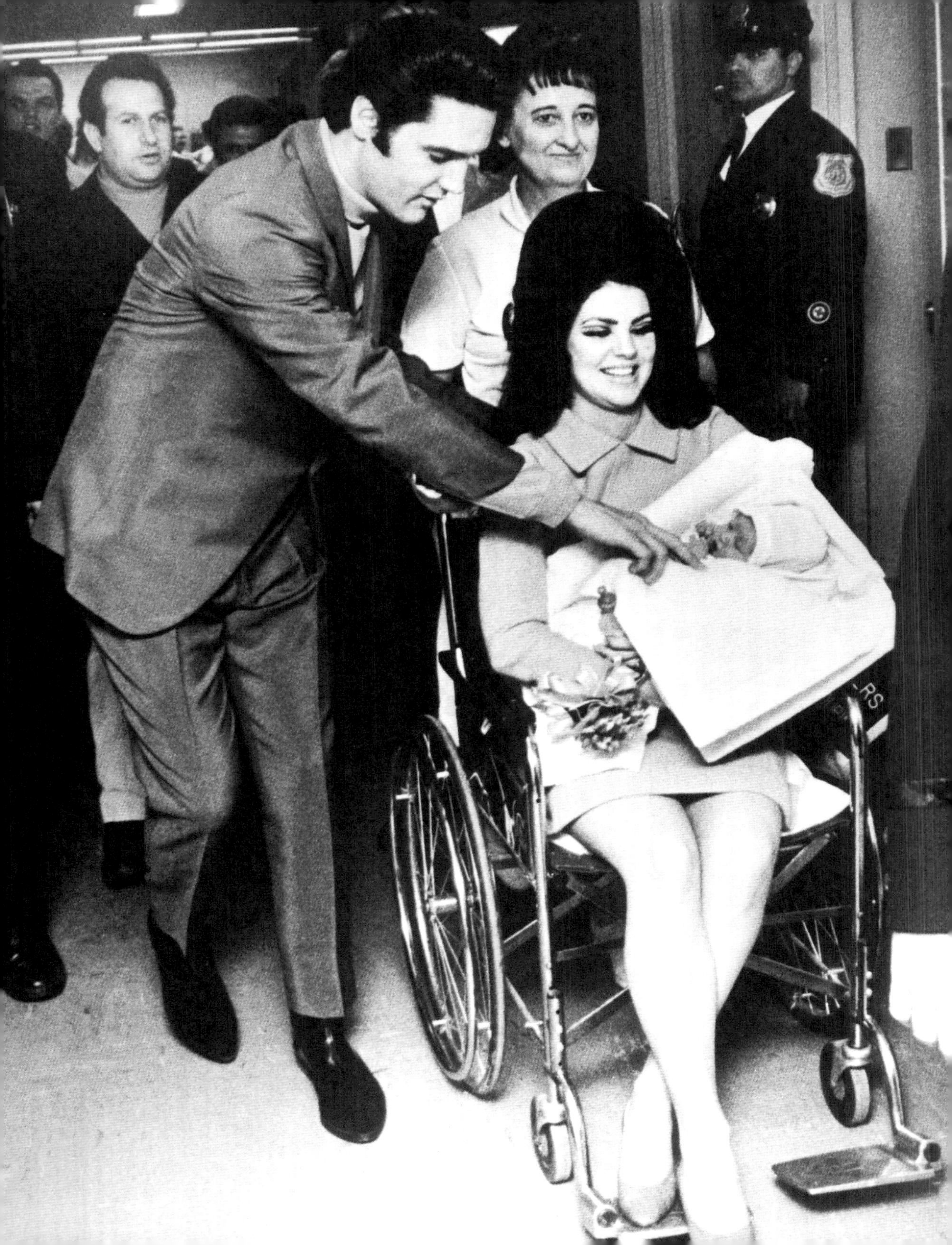

Elvis and Lisa Marie at Graceland

According to Jim Curtin, in *Elvis, Unknown Stories Behind the Legend*, when Lisa Marie's first baby tooth came out, Elvis left a $5 bill under her pillow. Priscilla had to tell Elvis off, because it was such a high amount at the time, with most kids only receiving 50 cents.

Elvis was so extravagant with gifts for his daughter, he even bought her a golf cart and a pony. While he showered Lisa Marie with love and material affection, Priscilla wrote, "Elvis wasn't a hands-on dad. And living at Graceland was difficult but I knew when I got married that he was going to have his guys around all the time. I could not domesticate Elvis, and I accepted that. He didn't really have that much to do with the practical stuff but I took naturally to becoming a mother. I thought, 'My God, this is a product of Elvis and me and I'm going to be there for her.' The moment you have the child, everything changes. It is terrifying and it is beautiful and it changed my life and it brought Elvis and me closer together."

Elvis takes Priscilla and Lisa Marie home from hospital, 1968

"I was the disciplinarian and there were times when Lisa didn't like it but you can't live life without boundaries. I was very subtle and very calm, and she knows this now. Lisa was four when Elvis and I divorced and we were very civil and we really wanted him to stay in her life and they spent plenty of time together. Elvis and I didn't suddenly not like each other."

Elvis had been reported to say proudly that Lisa Marie was a true Presley.

She loved performing in front of the mirror, singing into a hairbrush, and soaked up the attention and fuss from fans of Elvis. The young Lisa Marie also enjoyed posing for family pictures.

Elvis was very proud to be the father of his only child, Lisa Marie. He even named his private jet after her.

When Lisa Marie talked to television host Diane Sawyer, about her memories of Elvis as her father, she remembered him singing her lullabies, even waking her at odd hours, "Oh yeah, he'd always wake me up to sing in the middle of the night, get on the table and sing. I remember him as my dad, but he was a very exciting dad."

Elvis's private jet "Lisa Marie"

Lisa Marie performing onstage in 2012

Elvis at home with Lisa Marie and Priscilla

Lisa Marie with her mother, Priscilla, at a premiere in 1977

Both father and daughter had a passion for singing, and when Lisa Marie was old enough to learn lyrics to songs, she would try to impress her father with her renditions. Sometimes she learned his songs and later would famously film and sing digitally-managed duets with her father after his death, to mark anniversaries of his passing.

Lisa Marie was not baptized. Although Priscilla was raised a Catholic and Elvis a Baptist Christian, they had agreed she should decide herself.

She talked with Sawyer of what it was like to see Graceland, the rooms enshrined to Elvis and how it was when he died: "It's hard. It's also really comforting," she said. "I don't know if anyone has, you know, the place that they were raised, you know, held in a capsule like this. It's not often that you have that."

Lisa Marie described her awareness of his unhappiness, saying, "I think that he was in trouble. He was not happy. He was, you know, obviously crying out for help.

"If I was watching TV in my room, he'd come to my room and sort of stumble to my doorway and start to fall, and I had to go catch him. You know, things like that. And he'd try to pull himself out of it if he saw me, things like that."

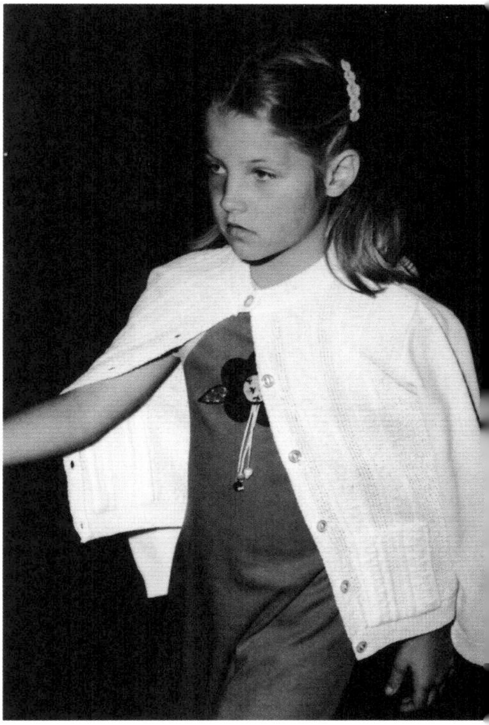

Lisa Marie aged nine in 1977

Elvis live onstage in 1975

Back-to-back performances began to tire Elvis

Sadly, she told Sawyer, she would say to him, "Don't die. Are you going to die?"

When Elvis collapsed, Lisa Marie saw the paramedics take his body away. Describing the event, she said she "couldn't really process what was happening" but did vividly recall the day of the public viewing of Elvis's body.

"I did a lot of strange things that day, because it didn't really settle in. I rode my golf cart. I ran around and smoked cigarettes at nine, in the guard shack somewhere. I was crazy. I don't know, I did, like, wacky things."

Lisa Marie inherited her father's looks, with her eyes and lips resembling his. The following excerpts from her interview with *Playboy* magazine are a fascinating insight into how Lisa Marie perceived Elvis as a father.

When asked how her parents' divorce affected her, when she was just five years old Lisa Marie replied, "When they divorced, I would go out on the road more and miss more school, which I liked. People say I didn't get to see him very much, but I was with him quite a bit. All of a sudden, a car would show up at school, and he was calling for me to go out on the road."

Following the divorce, Lisa Marie would spend time with him often at Graceland, she said of those times, "[Seeing her father was] Nocturnal: Go to bed at four or five a.m. and get up at two or three the next afternoon. It was always a lot of fun. There is not one bad memory. There was always a lot of energy and life in the house. He was very mischievous.

"The only two rooms upstairs in Graceland are mine and his. When he slept, he was a bear in hibernation."

And when asked further about her father's addiction to prescribed pills, she said, "I was aware of his demise. [Softly] His temper was getting worse, he was gaining weight, he was not happy. I saw him taking different pills, like a potpourri of capsules, but I didn't know what they were. He was obviously not in good shape. But he didn't want me to see that. So he would try to mask it for me.

"I was there when he died. I was there for most of the summer. I'm actually not going to go into his death, the day of, the whole thing. Just so you know."

Elvis Presley's funeral procession, 1977

Elvis meets President Nixon in 1970

In the *Ladies Home Journal* interview, not long after her divorce from Elvis, Priscilla said of having Lisa Marie, "Elvis and I were ecstatic over the birth of our daughter. If the baby had been a boy, we were going to name him John Barron. I liked the name Barron. It has a very strong feeling to it. But when it was a girl, we decided on Lisa Marie—for no special reason, only because it is a very feminine name.

"When the baby got a little older—she's five now—I started going out more with other women whose husbands were in Elvis's group; we'd go to the park, go shopping, or go out for lunch. If Elvis got time off, we'd take a trip, but we were seldom by ourselves. For instance, our stay in Hawaii was supposed to be a cozy family vacation. Elvis had finished filming *Blue Hawaii*, and he wanted to show me the islands. So we rented a bungalow with a private beach. But with an entourage of twelve people (each guy and his wife), how intimate can you become? I accepted it, but occasionally if I became resentful, Elvis would tease me out of it."

Regarding how Lisa Marie understood the divorce of her parents, Priscilla said,

"She thinks daddy is on a business trip so it works out. And Elvis is no absentee father. When he's on tour, he often calls her, and when he's in town, he sees her a lot. She spent last weekend with him, and I took her to watch him perform in Las Vegas for her birthday."

On her twenty-fifth birthday, Lisa Marie inherited the Graceland estate, estimated at that time to be worth $100 million.

Priscilla Presley and Elvis Presley in Hawaii, 1968

Lisa Marie inherited Graceland

The King is Back Again

Pictured during his performance at NBC studios, 1968

As if he had many lives, Elvis had a third return to musical success—his 1968 Comeback Special

After a lackluster few years filming a series of formulaic movies and experiencing a lack of creativity with his music, Elvis was keen to be born yet again. What followed was a powerful moment in Elvis's time as The King of Rock 'n' Roll.

The '68 *Comeback Special* was originally to be a Christmas show, but Elvis defied Parker's instructions and went with the director Steve Binder's suggestion that it be just like old times. Binders, who was also co-producing the show, had to convince Elvis the audience would respond to a rock 'n' roll, old school Elvis.

Ultimately very different from the proposed format Parker had arranged, it aired in December 1968, titled *Elvis*. The show featured a support band with a small audience and Elvis in tight black leather. It was NBC's highest rating show that season, with figures harking back to his first year of success, a total of 42 percent of the viewing audience.

Journalist Jon Landau of *Eye* magazine declared, "There is something magical about watching a man who has lost himself find his way back home. He sang with the kind of power people no longer expect of rock 'n' roll singers. He moved his body with a lack of pretension and effort that must have made Jim Morrison green with envy."

The single released to coincide with the TV special "If I Can Dream" hit the charts, climbing to number twelve. The album, the soundtrack to *Elvis*, hit the top ten.

Elvis during his '68
Comeback Special
on NBC

A series of recording sessions followed this positive reception. The sessions led to the much-loved *From Elvis in Memphis*, the first album unattached to an Elvis film in eight years. The album featured "In the Ghetto," which hit Number Three on the charts. Other hit singles that followed included "Suspicious Minds," "Don't Cry Daddy," and "Kentucky Rain."

In addition to the successful recording, Elvis was receiving offers for live performances from around the world. Come May, Vegas's International Hotel announced Elvis was scheduled to perform nearly sixty shows over a four-week period.

With a new band, led by guitarist James Burton, Elvis and Parker organized for the inclusion of two gospel groups, The Imperials and Sweet Inspirations. With his early history of lackluster performances in Vegas, Elvis was concerned. But Parker managed a massive PR program around his appearances and even flew in music journalists for the opening night.

The first gig held an audience of 2,200, many of whom were celebrities. When Elvis walked onstage without introduction, he was greeted with a standing ovation. Two more standing ovations followed. He was modest in his receipt of the praise that also followed. Elvis pointed to Fats Domino when a journalist addressed Elvis as The King. Elvis said, "That's the real King of Rock 'n' Roll."

Parker cemented Elvis's musical rebirth with a five-year contract with the International Hotel, for an annual earning of $800,000. He was to play every February and August. A short while later, Elvis released the double album *From Memphis to Vegas/From Vegas to Memphis*, including live performances from the hotel and the sound sessions. "Suspicious Minds" became his first American Number One in more than seven years. It was sadly to be his last.

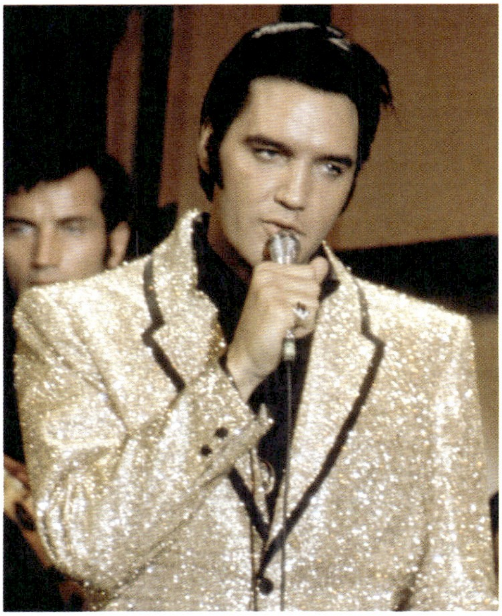

Elvis during another performance at NBC, 1968

Onstage at the International Hotel, Las Vegas, Nevada, summer 1969

ELVIS PRESL

Elvis Presley arrives in Hawaii for his televised concert

In early 1970, Elvis was performing two shows a night, over a long two-month period at the International Hotel. Another live album was issued from these appearances, called *On Stage*.

By late February, he had performed six record-breaking shows, with the highest attendance recorded at the Houston Astrodome. MGM continued to film documentary footage at the International, titling that release *Elvis: That's the Way It Is*. His jumpsuit-wearing appearances marked another shift in his metamorphosis as a performer.

It was at this time that Elvis was named one of the US Junior Chamber of Commerce's Ten Most Outstanding Young Men of the Nation in 1971. He was also the first rock star to be awarded the Lifetime Achievement Award (then known as the Bing Crosby Award) by the National Academy of Recording Arts and Sciences, the Grammy Award organization.

By this point, Elvis was touring the country, selling out venues, and frequently breaking box-office records. Over his lifetime, he performed a total of nearly 1,100 concerts. Having performed two benefit concerts for a television special, *Aloha From Hawaii*, Elvis was continuing to find form. Airing in January of 1973 to high ratings, the soundtrack reached Number Eight.

It was the first global concert satellite broadcast. Elvis was now reaching millions of viewers live across the globe.

From this show, Elvis's attire became iconic and instantly recognisable. American writer Bobbie Ann Mason said: "At the end of the show, when he spreads out his American Eagle cape, with the full stretched wings of the eagle studded on the back, he becomes a god figure."

Presley during a live performance at Honolulu International Center in Honolulu, Hawaii on January 14, 1973

Elvis Presley performing on the Elvis Comeback *TV special on June 27, 1968*

The Vegas Years

The costumes, the sellout performances, the relentless show schedule of Elvis's Vegas years

Following his '68 *Comeback Special*, Elvis wrapped up his movie contracts and returned to the stage in 1969. His last live show being the benefit concerts in Pearl Harbor and Honolulu, Hawaii in 1961, it would be eight years before he returned to live shows and to Vegas.

His arrival in Vegas did wonders for the city, and initially, for him, too. He attracted a new audience to Vegas, with much younger city folk travelling to The Strip to see Elvis perform. After almost a decade locked into dull movie deals he was bored with, Presley found his live shows in Vegas reinvigorated him. He was also feeling like he needed a reinvention.

Telling a journalist, "I've been away from people—real people—too long. Working for Hollywood was fine, and I've got no complaints about the way I was treated, but they put me on a production line. I was making films back-to-back, sometimes three a year, and although there was plenty of music in them, I had no say in what I sang or how I sang it.

"Whenever I tried to make a point, or change something, some guy in a suit would come over, surrounded by lawyers and accountants, and they'd tell me that I signed my name to a contract and I gotta do what they tell me. Well, I was a good boy and I didn't argue, because my mama always told me to mind my manners."

"We do two shows a night for five weeks. A lotta times we'll go upstairs and sing until daylight—gospel songs. We grew up with it . . . it more or less puts your mind at ease. It does mine."

—Elvis during Vegas live shows, taken from a 1972 taped interview used in MGM's documentary Elvis on Tour

Wearing black leather for his Comeback Special

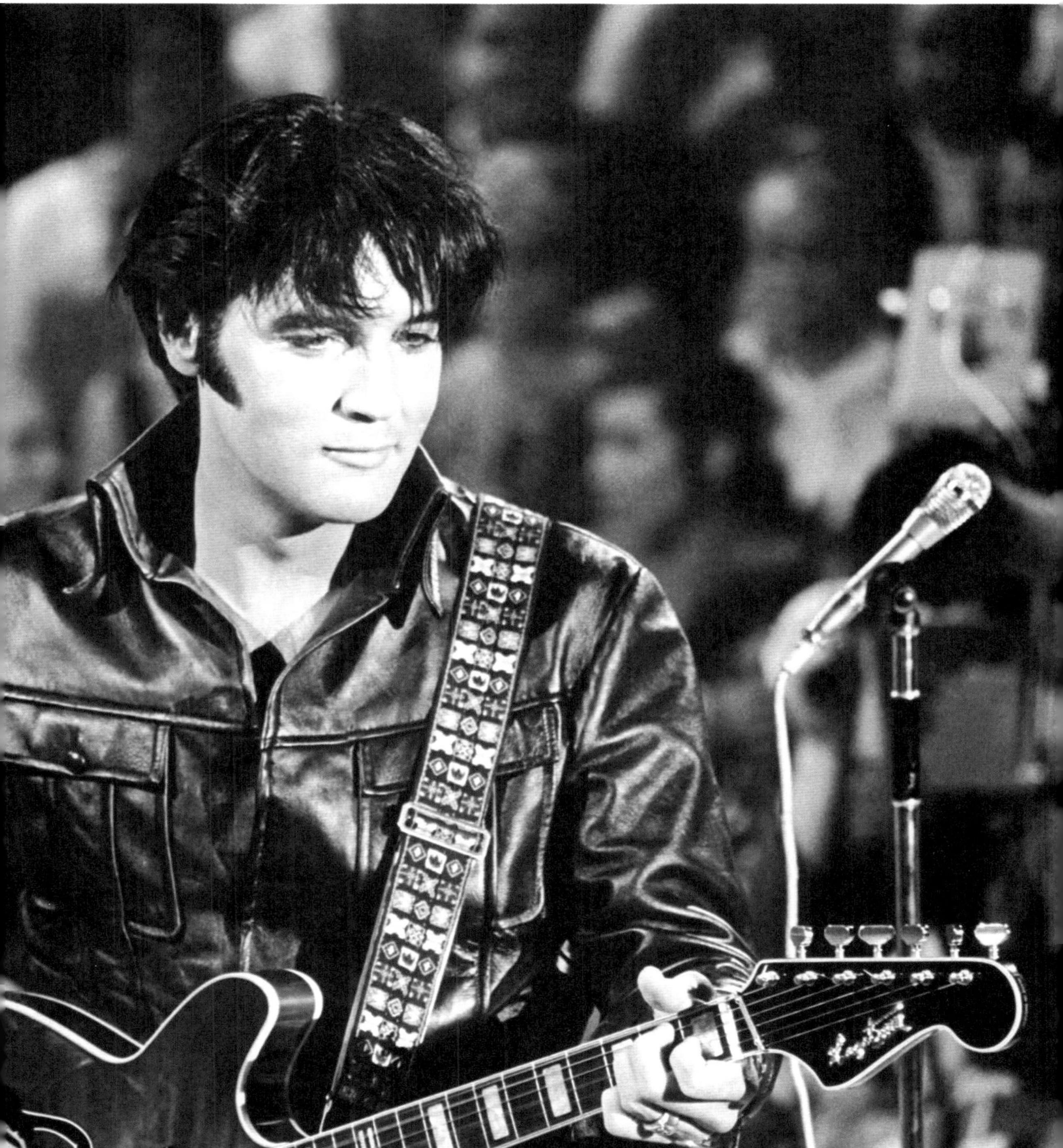

The International Hotel advertises performances by Elvis Presley

"But I was bored with movies, bored with the people, and bored with my life. I felt I'd sold my soul to the Devil. I look on today as the day I get back to doing the work that God put me on Earth to do. My big problem, though, is that maybe Vegas won't want to know me."

American songwriter Mike Stoller later told a BBC documentary team that, "There was a coolness factor, a hip factor. He brought something to Vegas that it needed."

Tom Jones told the same documentary, "Elvis wanted to prove a point after the movies. I was one of the few solo artists around who was still successful, so in 1968 he'd come to Vegas to watch me perform and see my body movements, which he had always been known for, too.

"He wanted to see and hear me firsthand to know whether audiences still wanted that sort of thing.

"He loved being Elvis Presley. There was no doubt about that. He loved it when he was great and who could blame him? But then I think he started to dislike himself. He lost his desire to be Elvis Presley."

Parker's wife, Loanne, said of Elvis, "He was the first entertainer to make a profit in the show room. Before that, the casinos used to subsidize the entertainment because they knew they'd get their money back at the tables. But Elvis changed all that and drew the big players in. The women were thrilled because they went to see the shows at night while their men were in the casino. Everyone was happy. When Elvis was in town, everything lit up."

Elvis came to watch Tom Jones in Las Vegas to pick up some fresh dance moves

From 1969 to 1976, Elvis performed to a very heavy concert schedule. Inevitably for Elvis, they were always sellout shows. His fans and supporters must have been keen—selling out 2,200 seats two times a day over a month. In what would now be considered too grueling a concert schedule for any performer, he was performing two concerts daily, usually one in the afternoon and the following as late as midnight. What followed was to seriously impact his physical and mental health and wellbeing.

Opening in the summer of '69, his four-week gig featured fifty-seven shows, which broke attendance records. Incredibly, *Newsweek* reported not just positive press reviews, but a record-breaking Las Vegas show attendance of 101,509 and another Vegas record of gross sales at $1.5 million.

Rumor has it that Elvis celebrated the news by giving a diamond-studded Rolex watch to each of his thirty members of his entourage and bought fourteen Cadillacs, one for each of his close friends.

Elvis's live show then went on the road in the 70s, where he continued to break box office records. At Madison Square Garden, Elvis performed four sold-out shows in 1972. Between 1969 and 1977, Elvis clocked up almost 1,100 live performances.

Understanding how popular and successful his shows were, it is surprising to learn of how nervous and full of self-doubt Elvis would be about performing. From observers at the International Hotel show on July 31, 1969, he paced back and forth nervously.

However, as the audience's rumble simmered down to a quiet hush, and the orchestra played, Elvis ruled the stage and performed an incredible show.

Elvis performing on NBC in June 1968

Elvis Presley onstage during his 1972 Madison Square Garden Concert

It was during these Vegas years that Elvis began wearing elaborate costumes. Perhaps to disguise his growing insecurities and odd behavior, the costumes would be a distraction. Whatever his motivation for wearing them, they were fitting of the Vegas setting. With broad shoulders, he had costumes designed with capes and V-cuts from his neck to his waist. He wore gold chains and medallions and was generally keen on what Priscilla called "flashy" jewelery.

Elvis's home-town friend, Jerry Schilling, said of the outfits, "Elvis and all of us became Vegas-ized. Nothing he did, was in moderation. If a few sequins looked good on his jumpsuit in the lights, then at the next show there had to be more. If a high collar worked for him, the collars kept getting higher. The belt buckles kept getting bigger.

"As the years went on in Vegas, so did the wardrobe. Elvis was fanatical about his clothes."

As his health declined with his increase of prescription drugs, Elvis began to put on more and more weight. His now trademark jumpsuits had to be remade each time Elvis arrived in Vegas. But, his costume maker Gene Doucette recalls, "His body made a perfect 'V.' He went from wide shoulders down to perfect hips and you can't ask for more than that when you are trying to design a sexy outfit for a stage presentation.

"His clothes became as integral a part of Elvis as his music, his lighting and his whole show. With all the stones on them, the clothes were really heavy, perhaps adding 25–30lbs extra for him to carry. And all the time the costumes were becoming ever more flamboyant."

Observers could see that as Elvis's behavior worsened, he became more and more preoccupied with the clothes he wore on stage. He asked for bigger collars, more rhinestones.

His behavior worsened onstage, too. Guests noticed he slurred his words, would ramble and rant to the audience, and forget the lyrics to his songs, those he had sung over and over many times before.

Elvis sitting down onstage, 1975

Performing in his signature white, studded suit

Presley during a live performance at Honolulu International Center in Hawaii

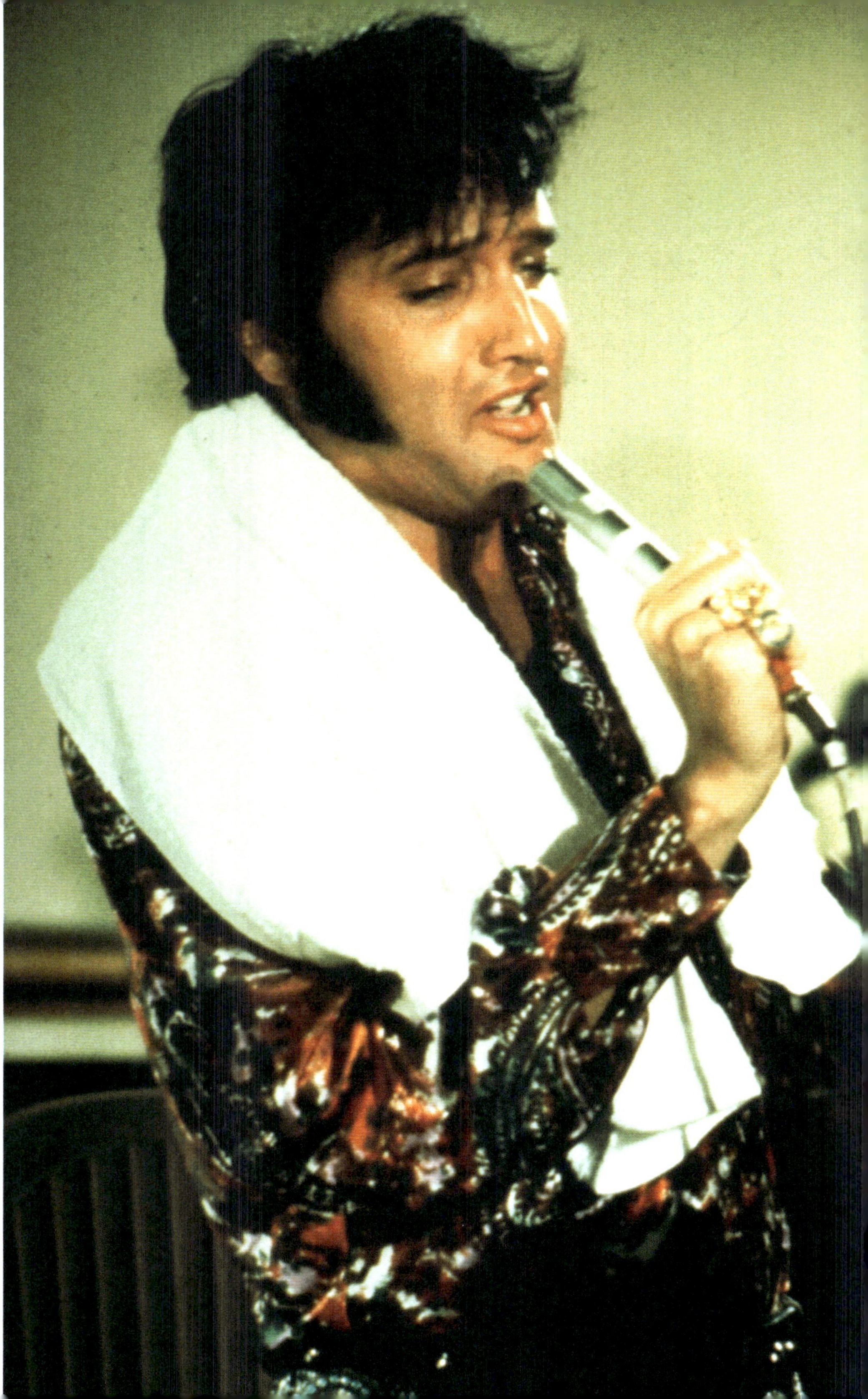

Elvis rehearses in 1973

Apparently, Elvis had five different doctors prescribing drugs to him, and because of patient-doctor confidentiality, none of them knew what each other were prescribing or had any contact with each other to understand the impact the various pills were having together.

Elvis is parodied in a sketch show in 1976

Several people recall Elvis having an icy wake-up call from Parker to rouse him from a pill-induced slumber before one of his shows. By the early seventies, Elvis was taking painkillers, amphetamines, barbiturates and medication for a sinus problem. This prescription cocktail must have had grave affects on his health.

After a while, Elvis became less interested in hiding the pills and covering up his addiction.

Linda Thompson, his girlfriend after his divorce from Priscilla recalled "One night I saw all these prescription bottles on his bedside table. I said, 'Elvis, are you sick?' He said, 'No, no, honey, I had a little sore throat.'

"He needed a lot of care, physically and emotionally. There were times he was my baby, other times my brother, my lover, or just my friend. He would shower gifts—cars, diamonds, even houses—on friends and strangers alike. He was so incredibly generous and we would call him either crazy or a fallen angel."

In a 1974 concert at the Hilton, Elvis was surreptitiously recorded ranting onstage to his fans about various rumors and people in his life. Later released by a Las Vegas news team and reported by George Knapp, a journalist with Eyewitness News I-TEAM, who are a television investigative unit in southern Nevada, the recording has been variously interpreted as sad and shocking.

It was reported that Elvis appeared disoriented and started talking about the rumors regarding his drug use. The following quotes are excerpts from the recording, reported by Knapp, and his news team:

"I hear rumors flying around—I got sick in the hospital. In this day and time you can't even get sick. You are strung out. By god I'll tell you something, I have never been strung out in my life, except on music. I got sick that one night, I had a hundred and two temperature, and they wouldn't let me perform, from three different sources I heard I was strung out on heroin. I swear to god, hotel employees, jack, bellboys, freaks who carry that luggage up to your room, people, you know maids. And I was sick. But all across town, strung out."

According to Knapp and his team, Priscilla was in the audience during this particular show, and the following excerpt from the recording is about her: ". . . my ex-wife Priscilla. She's right here. Honey, stand up . . . turn around, let them see you . . . boy she's a beautiful chick, you know, (. . .). Now my little daughter Lisa Marie, she's six years old, look at her jump up. Pull your dress down Lisa, pull your dress down before you jump up like that. And at the same booth is my girlfriend Sheila. Stand up Sheila, turn completely around. . . ."

"No the thing I'm tryin to get across, we're the best of friends, always has been. Our divorce came about not because of another man or another woman but because of circumstances involving my career. I was traveling too much . . . after the settlement, it came out about two million dollars . . . after that I got her a mink coat. She got me, listen to this, tonight, a $42,000 Rolls Royce. That's the type of relationship we have. . . ."

Performing live in 1976

Elvis Presley arrives at the Hilton Inn after a concert in 1974

Then Elvis referred to Priscilla's new boyfriend Mike Stone.

Elvis continued, "She likes this Stutz that I have. It's not a car it's a Stutz, no it's called a stud. A Stutz, and she likes the stud . . . Mike Stone ain't no stud, so forget it, . . ."

In another Vegas show, it was reported that four men attempted to attack Elvis. As security men rushed the stage, Elvis employed his karate skills and managed to remove one of the attackers himself.

There were also rumors he believed that this attack was organized by Priscilla's boyfriend Stone and that Elvis was paranoid about Stone. There were even stories that Elvis had asked his bodyguards to check out the possibility of a contract killing of Stone, before Elvis changed his mind. These stories were not substantiated, but it was widely agreed Elvis was affected by, and under the influence of, drugs during his Vegas years.

Ironically, he was previously reported to have been very anti-drugs and alcohol, presumably because he had known family members to be alcohol dependent. His awareness of the dangers of prescription drugs was not as strong.

Indeed, to some it seemed that Elvis's upbringing meant he had very strong ideas of right and wrong, but little worldliness that would help him choose right and wrong for himself.

His purist views were obvious when the hotel casino offered Elvis thousands of dollars worth of gambling chips every day, which he refused because of his religious beliefs.

In 1976, Elvis finished his 837th and final show in Vegas, going home to Graceland.

"He definitely believed he had been blessed by God. It wasn't just an accident—he had been picked out. He used to question it, though. 'Why me?' he would say."
—Tom Jones on Elvis Presley

1976 was a busy year for live performances

Elvis performing in Concert at the Philadelphia Spectrum, 1976

Memphis Mafia

The tight friendship circle Elvis kept from his late teens to his death

In his childhood and adolescence, Elvis was unpopular with his peers, both male and female. He struggled to get the attention of girls, and boys considered him awkward, a loner, and too much of a "mama's boy." So when he found fame and fortune in his late teens and early twenties, Elvis's popularity must have come as a shock.

He felt safe with people of his own kind, with similar backgrounds and upbringing to his. He was not used to associating with the rich and famous in the music industry and Hollywood.

For the first time, Elvis headed up a large group of friends, who wanted to be with him. According to biographers, the group of friends who would later be dubbed The Memphis Mafia began with Elvis's first cousins Junior and Gene Smith. Along with a high school friend, Red West, they went everywhere with Elvis.

The Memphis Mafia would later grow in numbers, although the inner circle only ever included one woman. Judy Spreckels became Elvis's confidante and said that she "was with him and the guys all the time."

"There wasn't a crowd then, just a few guys… [being his friend] had nothing to do with being a yes man for him and obviously he trusted me."

It was during the early 1960s that Elvis's close circle of friends, who he kept right up until his death, were named the 'Memphis Mafia'. The name came from a journalist who observed their dark suits and sunglasses, which were apparently requested by Elvis in order that they all look respectable. Apparently, the friends thought it an amusing title and, along with Elvis, did not object to it.

As the story was told, it happened when the friends arrived at a hotel by black limousine and someone in the crowd yelled, "Who are they, the Mafia?"

Who were the Memphis Mafia?

Elvis Presley arriving with bodyguard Red West

Elvis looks in pain onstage

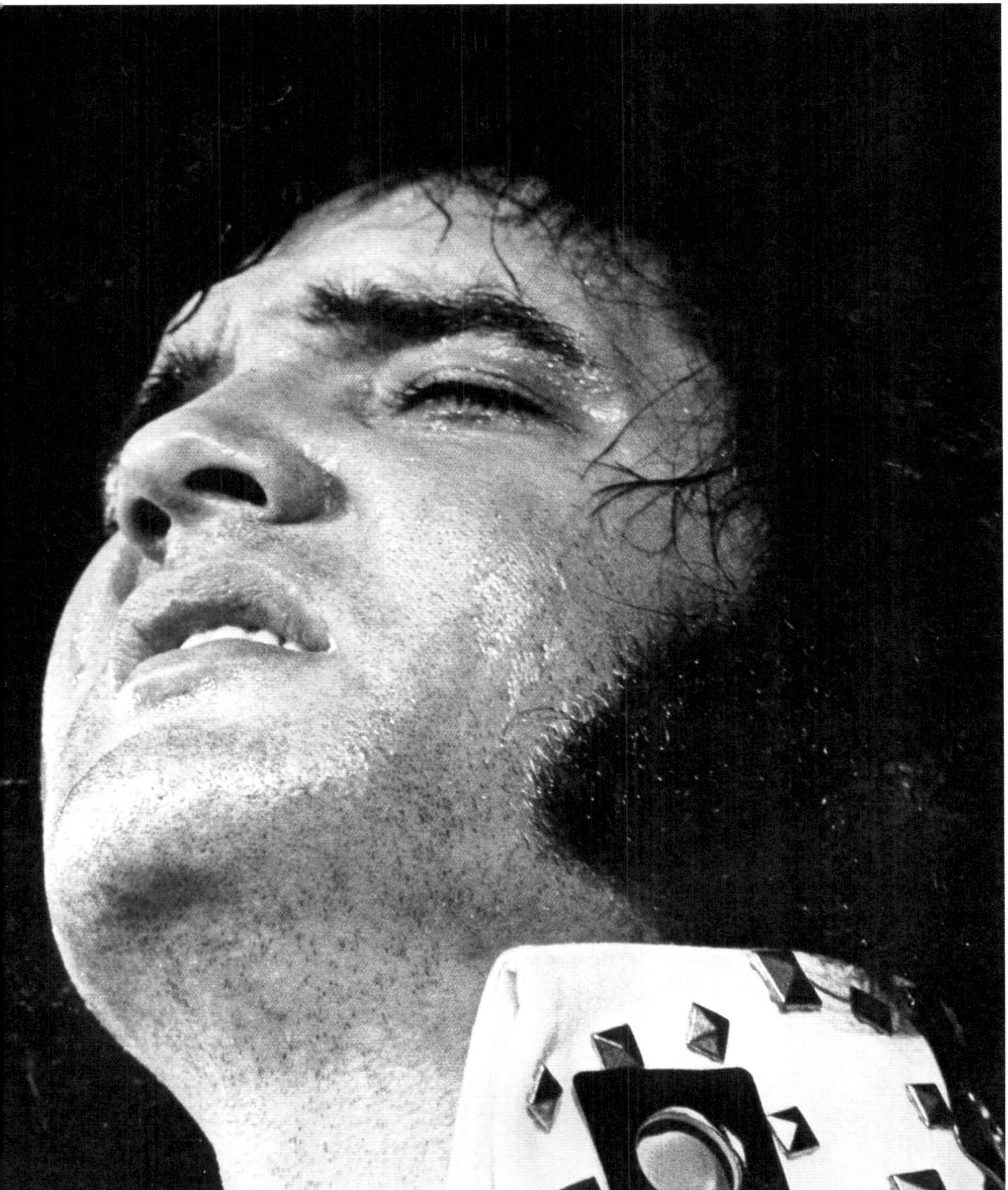

Marty Lacker was one of the original circle. He met Elvis as a teenager, as he went to the same high school as Elvis, in his final year. He was one of two best men at Elvis's wedding and was considered Elvis's right hand man. He said of the group, "Most of the guys had responsibilities and they were far from leeches, hangers on or whatever else they were called. They all had jobs to do so that Elvis could do his and as far as being there for the money, that's laughable because there really wasn't much in that area to be there for. Most of us were not there for the money, we were there because we all cared about Elvis and each other like brothers."

In late 1971, Lacker arranged for the Memphis City Council to rename Highway 51, which runs in front of Graceland, as Elvis Presley Boulevard. He was also responsible, along with Parker, for arranging the Elvis recording at American Studios in 1969 that basically brought Elvis back to the top of the charts. He was close to Elvis from 1957 until he died in 1977.

Gene Smith was Elvis's cousin, and as part belonging to a close family, they had a close friendship growing up together. Elvis considered Smith to be a very important person in his life, and would often travel with him. Many have said Smith went everywhere with Elvis. It was reported that the cousins suffered a disagreement in the early sixties, but would later come together and spend time at Graceland with each other.

Junior Smith was another cousin, who sadly became disabled during the Korean War. When Elvis got a call that Junior had died, he took the news badly.

Elvis posing in a police uniform, Presley kept friends in the police force, particularly the narcotics department

Elvis Presley during a press conference after his first performance at the International Hotel in Las Vegas, Nevada on August 1, 1969

Billy Smith, another cousin of Elvis's who made in into his close-knit circle, was the youngest of the group and reportedly Elvis's favorite. A loyal friend and constant companion, Billy Smith was good to Elvis right to the end of Elvis's life.

George Klein was another fellow graduate of Humes High School in 1953. When George started working in radio, he blossomed into one of Memphis's most popular DJs. Elvis said of Klein, "George will be my friend forever."

Lamar Fike began working for Elvis in 1957. Fike had a good sense of humor and while working for Elvis became a good friend, often traveling with him on tour and working as his lighting director.

Larry Geller joined Elvis's inner circle when he became his hairdresser in 1964. He was different from Elvis's other friends, being a spiritual person who encouraged Elvis to read about religion, spirituality, and mysticism. He peaked Elvis's curiosity, which was no surprise considering his religious start to life and the unique experiences he had in life, "I mean there has to be a purpose . . . there's got to be a reason . . . why I was chosen to be Elvis Presley. . . . I swear to God, no one knows how lonely I get. And how empty I really feel."

Joe Esposito, who acted as Elvis's road manager and personal aide for nearly seventeen years, handled money and cross-referenced the extensive travel arrangements. He said, "It was a party like you wouldn't believe. Go to a different show every night, then pick up a bunch of women afterwards, go party the next night. Go to the lounges, see Fats Domino, Della Reese, Jackie Wilson, The Four Aces, the Dominoes—all the old acts. We'd stay there and never sleep, we were all taking pills just so we could keep up with each other." Esposito was the other best man at Elvis's wedding.

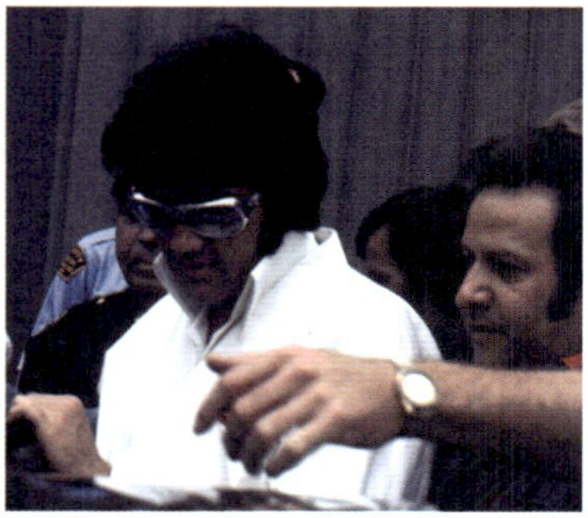

Elvis Presley and Joe Esposito (right) leaving JFK

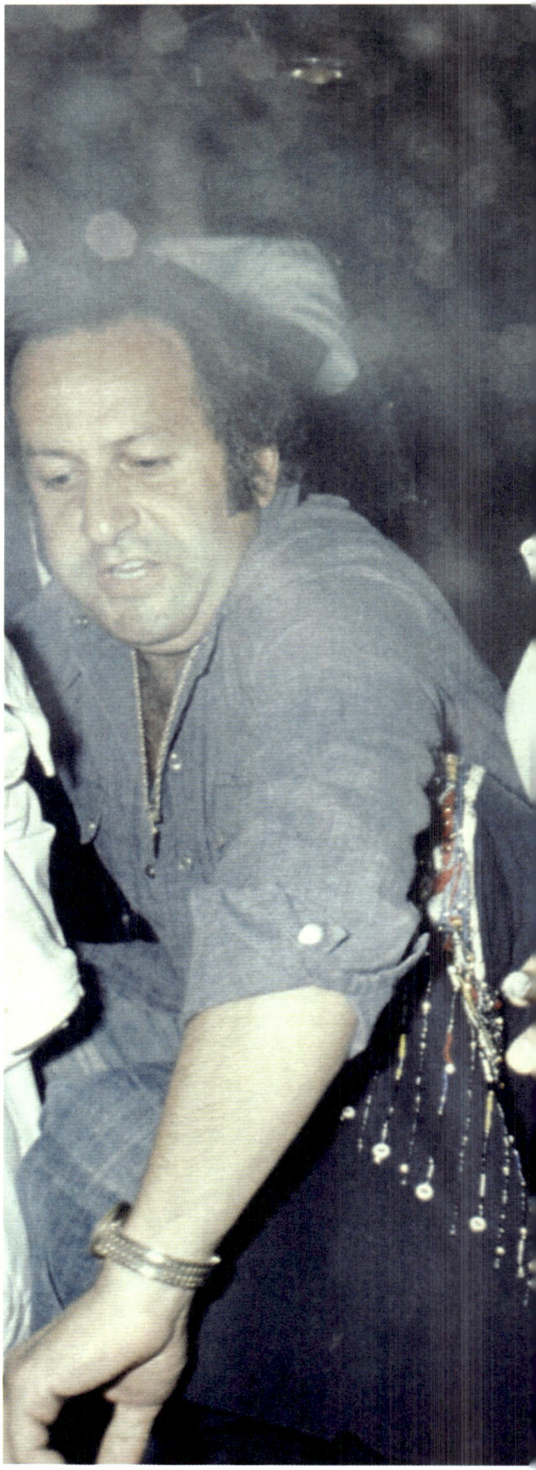

Joe Esposito, Elvis Presley, and Goodman leaving a hotel

Elvis and his entourage, 1970

Over the years, many people would become involved with the Memphis Mafia, but the most prominent members in Elvis's later years are widely acknowledged to be (in no particular order) Red West, Sonny West, Marty Lacker, Billy Smith, Gene Smith, Joe Esposito, Nick Adams, Lamar Fike, Alan Fortas, Richard Davis, Dave Hebler, Al Strada, stepbrothers David and Billy Stanley, Larry Geller, Charlie Hodge, and Jerry Schilling.

Samuel Roy says that "Elvis's bodyguards, Red and Sonny West and Dave Hebler, apparently loved Elvis—especially Red; these bodyguards showed loyalty to Elvis and demonstrated it in the ultimate test. When bullets were apparently fired at Elvis in Las Vegas, the bodyguards threw themselves in front of Elvis, forming a shield to protect him." The author adds that the people who surrounded Presley "lived, for the most part, in isolation from the rest of the world, losing touch with every reality except that of his 'cult' and his power."

According to Presley expert Elaine Dundy, "Of all Elvis's new friends, Nick Adams, by background and temperament the most insecure, was also his closest." Guralnick says that the singer "was hanging out more and more with Nick and his friends" and that Elvis was glad Parker "liked Nick." June Wilkinson also confirms that the singer "had an entourage who spoke with Southern accents. The only one I remember was Nick Adams, the actor."

Many of his friends from Memphis worked with Elvis and were employed by his estate. For some of them, it may have been the only way out of the poverty they grew up in. By many accounts, most of the friends were fiercely loyal to Elvis, although this was challenged by many in later years as various Memphis Mafia members revealed stories about Elvis for well paid tell-all books that went on to be published.

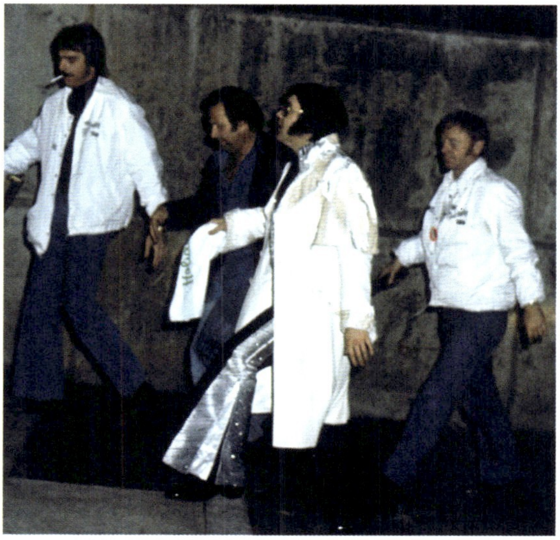

Elvis arrives at the Hilton Inn with his bodyguards in 1976

Elvis surrounded by bodyguards, 1975

By writer Patrick Humphries' account, they "acted as Elvis's bodyguards, babysitters, drug procurers, girl-getters, mates and car buyers."

". . . various members of the Memphis Mafia had . . . played vital roles in keeping Elvis's numerous dirty secrets out of the public eye. A couple of them had been arrested with false prescriptions attempting to collect drugs for Elvis, quite a few had taken physical hits in the service of protecting Elvis and none were paid more than $500 a week. For that they were often shouted at, abused and belittled by the King when he felt like it."

By other accounts, writers like Jerry Eden claim they were only it in for the money, saying it made him "sick to see Elvis's two-faced cousins, members of the so-called Memphis Mafia, who hung around him for the money, clothes, cars, and leftover girls."

"[They] were mostly his second and third cousins from Mississippi. With the exception of a couple of the guys, like Charlie Hodge and Red West, most of his friends were simply ignorant hillbillies out to get everything they could from him. . . . They had a real sweet thing going that's for sure. They called themselves bodyguards, but in reality they were only flunkies falling over each other to kiss El's ass."

Author Jerry Eden claims there was no love lost between Priscilla and the group of men, "When Priscilla came on the scene, she made them move out of Graceland, keeping just a couple of them in the house to act as bodyguards."

Many reported the negative influence this circle of friends had on Elvis, including Elvis's pianist Tony Brown. Brown saw Elvis regularly during the last two years of his life and said of his declining health and wellbeing, "But we all knew it was hopeless because Elvis was surrounded by that little circle of people . . . all those so-called friends."

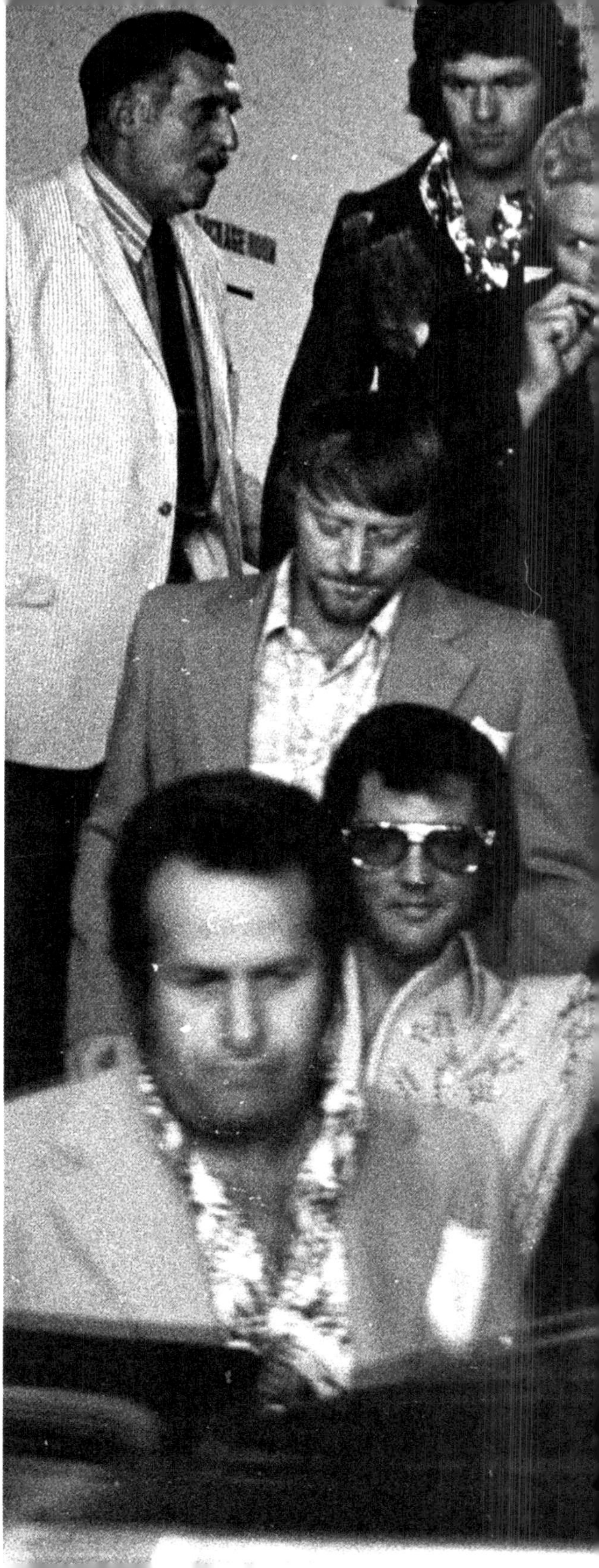

Elvis leaves the Hilton Hotel with his bodyguards in June 1972

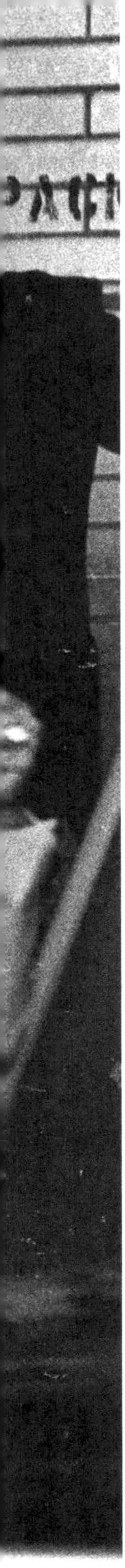

Elvis and his entourage driving out of Graceland, 1970

Elvis Presley polishes his first, of many, Cadillacs in 1956

According to biographer Peter Guralnick, "Hollywood was just an open invitation to party all night long. Sometimes they would hang out with Sammy Davis, Jr., or check out Bobby Darin at the Cloister. Nick Adams and his gang came by the suite all the time, not to mention the eccentric actor Billy Murphy . . ."

When Buzz Cason, a backup singer for Elvis, asked Lamar Fike how Elvis managed to party every night, Fike replied, "A little somethin' to get down and a little something to get up." Sadly, Elvis's addiction was obvious to his friends and either they did not, would not, or could not help him with it.

The group of friends famously also used the acronym TCB, which stood for Taking Care of Business. The circle of friends was given gold necklaces with TCB and Elvis had his private jet painted with the initials. Elvis, who bought them new Cadillacs and houses for wedding gifts, often gifted the friends generously.

The group, who would remain loyal to Elvis, was often criticized and doubted by journalists in particular. Journalist John Harris said, "it was no wonder that as he slid into addiction and torpor, no one raised the alarm: to them, Elvis was the bank, and it had to remain open."

Whether or not the group was lecherous and after Elvis's money, they certainly had some fun and mischievous times together. Stories abound regarding what the Memphis Mafia got up to. Again, without evidence, there were stories about the Mafia playing key roles in finding girls for Elvis, and for themselves.

Elvis Presley and singer Sammy Davis, Jr. backstage in Elvis's dressing room, opening night at the Showroom International Hotel on August 10, 1970

One of Parker's assistants, Byron Raphael, claimed he also had this role to fulfill. According to Raphael, the actress Natalie Wood felt rejected by Elvis, who would not have sexual intercourse with her. She then said to the Memphis Mafia that she "was not the only one to think Elvis and the guys might be homosexual, especially since Elvis often wore pancake makeup and mascara offstage to accentuate his brooding intensity, à la Tony Curtis and Rudolph Valentino, his favorite movie actors."

The loyalty of some of the members of the Memphis Mafia was questionable later in Elvis's life. In 1977, the West cousins joined with Dave Hebler to write an exposé on Elvis, which was dubbed *The Bodyguard Book*. It is generally thought they cared no longer for their loyalty to Elvis after Vernon, Elvis's father, fired the trio following what he considered to be rough handling in their roles as bodyguards.

It was said that Vernon Presley gave the reasons for their dismissal and delivered the news, saying that they had received complaints about how the bodyguards had reacted to fans as part of their role in protecting Elvis, and that Elvis's expenses were mounting.

The Wests were given a few weeks pay as severance and after they requested to speak with Elvis, he refused. It was reported they were upset about this, especially as they had worked for and been a part of Elvis's inner circle for twenty years. Elvis was said to be angry and hurt that the book was coming out. Titled *Elvis: What Happened?* it revealed Elvis's drug abuse and private stories about The King of Rock 'n' Roll.

Elvis and his father pictured after his first Las Vegas performance in 1969

Elvis performing on TV in 1968

Parker attempted to settle with the trio for a large monetary amount, but could not reach agreement. It was later said that they also tried to offer the publishers a settlement amount, which also did not work out.

When the trio held press conferences about the book launch, they claimed they wrote it to help Elvis understand the effect his medication addiction was having, to help him to seek help, and get clean from the addiction.

Elvis's youngest stepbrother recalled Elvis "was devastated by the book. Here were his close friends who had written serious stuff that would affect his life. He felt betrayed. Red was honest with Elvis about his medication problems and I think this was one of the reasons he was fired. For the guys they were fired, but not by Elvis. That must have hurt."

To many, it was unfortunate that several members of Elvis's inner circle would later pen a book, *Revelations from the Memphis Mafia*, where many unsavory stories about Elvis and the members of the Memphis Mafia would surface, who were sometimes rumored to be gay themselves, more than once insisted that the "gay rumors" that "got going when Elvis started hanging out with Nick Adams" were false, suggesting that it was not uncommon for gay men to be attracted to Presley, but that he was "prejudiced about homosexuals."

Much later, in 2007, Sonny West wrote and published *Elvis: Still Takin' Care of Business*, which was described as a gentler, kinder portrayal of life and friendship with the King.

In an interview with The Elvis Info Net website, Billy Smith talked of the inner circle known as the Memphis Mafia, of Elvis and their time together.

"I do remember him singing a lot for the family and different ones. He always had a love for music even at a very young age. Very early on I remember once when Elvis pulled me out of a garbage can! I fell in head first. I was little, and I was trying to get some bananas out that the man from the fruit stand had thrown away. Elvis saw me as he passed and pulled me out!

"Elvis was always my hero. And we were always close, even with the eight year age difference. He always looked after me, and I always wanted to be with him.

"I was always close to Elvis even as a young child. He always seemed to want me around him and was very protective of me. I always loved Elvis very much and would do just about anything to please him and be with him. We could talk about anything, and we did! He felt comfortable with me and trusted me. At least, he always told me he did.

"When he was sick, I usually stayed with him. I usually went to the hospital and stayed with him there. I had so much respect for him. He did a lot for me and my family in the early years and for my family in the later years. He always told me that he loved me. Maybe it's because I was where he was before it all happened, and that was the link. . . we were family. He was my hero."

Colonel Parker circa 1970

NOW!
ELVIS
FOR EASTER
ELVIS
JOSHUA FIT THE BATTLE
KNOWN ONLY TO HIM
2 GREAT SINGLES
ON RCA VICTOR

On Larry Geller's version of events with Elvis, Smith said,

"Larry Geller was okay. I don't agree with some of the tales he tells, but Larry was there for a while. He seems to remember his importance more than some of the other guys remember it. But, why bust his bubble. As I said, everyone had a job to do. Larry was his hairdresser.

"I was with him on many of the recording sessions. "The Memphis Mafia" was with Elvis almost twenty-four hours a day, at least one or two of them. And, in the early days, they lived with him."

Elvis Info Net also secured an interview with Lamar Fike, who revealed the following in response to various questions about their time together as part of the Memphis Mafia.

"The fun times outweigh the sad. Looking back just about every situation had its funny moments. We lived life to the fullest and the fun flowed from this.

"You've got to understand, Elvis was only human even if many want to sanctify him to a higher level. On an emotional level he was no different to you or I . . . he had feelings, strong feelings, and he was searching for what eludes so many of us, inner fulfillment and inner peace."

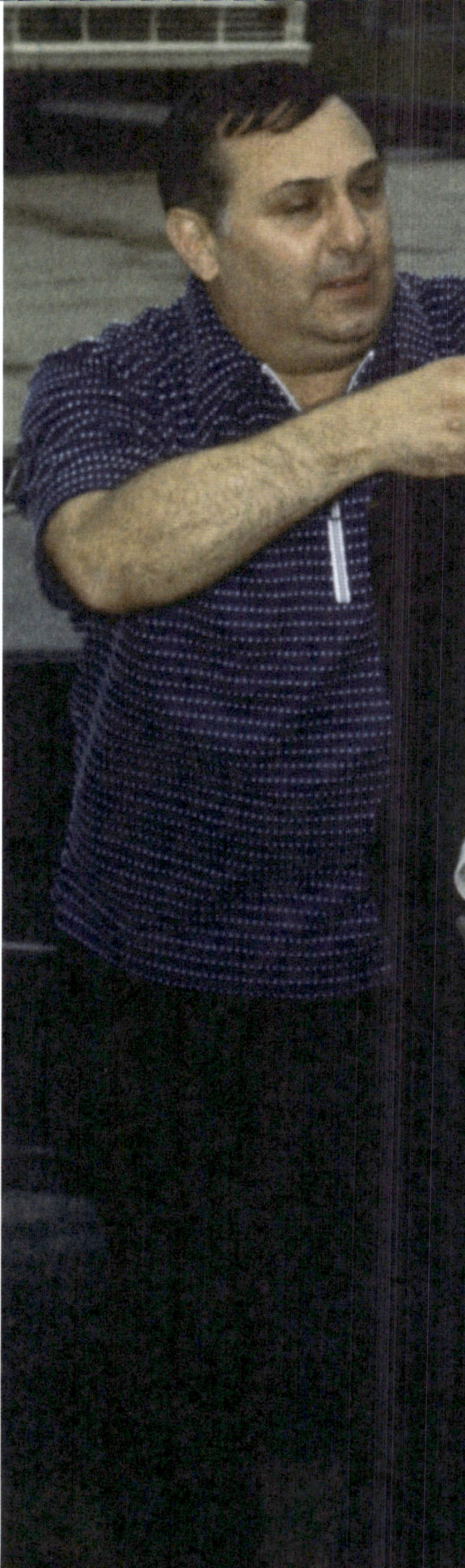

Elvis with his bodyguards after a concert in 1974

ELVIS
194

The Later Years

The years most Elvis fans would prefer to forget, Elvis's health and wellbeing declines while he continues his demanding tours

It could be said of Elvis that he was fortunate enough to have experienced two or even three careers. After a very quick ride to success as the King of Rock 'n' Roll, he returned from two years of Army duty, which at the time was a very long period between albums. Then after finding critical acclaim again with *Elvis is Back!* he suffered from a slow, grinding progression of films that bored his fans toward the end, just as it did him. He uniquely had another famous comeback in 1968, and was to become more popular than he was before.

His fan base was huge, with Elvis fellowship becoming almost cult-like. And yet, Elvis seemed to doubt himself more and more. Like most people, Elvis was full of contradictions. He was self-confident and enjoyed being liked and popular, but at the same time he was riddled with self-doubt and insecurity, with a deep need to be liked.

While outwardly charming and accepting of his fame, even describing autograph requests as something he had grown used to, his behavior became increasingly paranoid and private. He was reported to have become mistrustful of the general public, and was known to rent out cinemas in order to watch a film peacefully, as well as amusement parks at nighttime.

It seemed everything Elvis did was in excess. When he was a young boy, he was unpopular with the girls. So when he became famous and had attained sex symbol status, he had a number of women at any one time. He had affairs while he had girlfriends; he had affairs while he was married.

Elvis performs in one of his last concerts in 1977

Above and opposite; Presley kept slim with diet and exercise while filming during the early 1960s

Elvis Presley visits President Richard Nixon on December 21, 1970 at the White House in Washington, D.C.

Likewise, his relationships with men were in excess. When he was viewed as a "mama's boy" and was unpopular at school, Elvis did not have many friends. As his success increased and he rose to fame and fortune, Elvis kept as many friends close as he could, even inviting them to live with him at Graceland and going on tour with him. The Memphis Mafia was a much larger, more involved version of Sinatra's famous Rat Pack.

It seems that following his introduction to amphetamines while in the Army, Elvis became increasingly dependent on them in his later years, and certainly while performing in Las Vegas. While not confirmed, he was rumored to be abusing pharmaceutical drugs, barbiturates, tranquilizers, and amphetamines. It was also said that he had tried prescription pills as young as in his teens, and yet he was outwardly and outspokenly adverse to recreational drugs and alcohol.

Indeed, he would state that he rejected drugs and alcohol, and it would appear that he never drank or used so-called recreational drugs. However, he was obviously unaware of the dependency linked to over-the-counter drugs and amphetamines.

Because of his outspoken values on recreational drugs, and having been known to denounce them to fellow celebrities, President Nixon at the White House ironically awarded him an honorary Drug Enforcement Administration Agent's Badge.

Sadly, the recording released of him ranting onstage in Vegas and the witnessed performances of him rambling between songs showed his deterioration.

And just as with drugs, Elvis's relationship with food and his weight went from one extreme to another. At the height of his fame, when he was filming an average of two movies a year, he had to keep a close eye on his weight, his food consumption, and exercise, in order to keep slim for the camera.

Not long after his contract for the movies ended and Elvis found freedom in his career again, he began to overeat—he loved sweets and puddings. His weight soon ballooned with the bloating, a side effect from the prescription drugs. He was also growing obese and his health declined quite rapidly.

His work schedule was another extreme. Elvis went from cultivating a two-way artistic music relationship with Sam Phillips at Sun Records to what could be interpreted by outsiders as a one-way, commercial business relationship with his manager Colonel Parker. Parker continued to push schedules, demands, and financial gain from Elvis, locking him into long contracts with first his movies, and then ironically, again with the Vegas years.

The frantic tour schedules did not help. And the overly generous deal signed with Parker meant Elvis was tied into his commitment to Parker's arrangements. It was said that Parker suffered a gambling addiction and had also managed a very complex deal with RCA, which meant Elvis did not receive royalties.

Additional financial pressure came from Elvis's father, who was managing his finances, and not particularly well, by accounts. The financial outlook for Elvis, with his expensive homes and extremely generous way with gifts for friends and family, was not positive. It was likely this had an impact on Elvis's state of mind and happiness.

He came from nothing, a poor Tupelo kid who lived his later years in extravagance, wealth, and privilege. And yet, not one of these areas of his life of excess—fame, fortune, career, women, friendship, and health—brought him happiness or fulfillment.

What was life like for Elvis in his later years?

Rolex given to Elvis Presley by Colonel Tom Parker is shown at Christie's on November 23, 2012 in London, England. Estimated at $9,000–£12,000

Elvis Presley confers with Colonel Tom Parker on the set of one of his films

Again, Elvis lived his life with contradiction and so his later years were paradoxical. Finding fame as the rebel rock 'n' roller, The King would end up closing his career and his life on the well-established entertainment circuit of Las Vegas.

The rebellious man dubbed the King of Rock 'n' Roll was raised with an earnest, polite, religious, upbringing. He would talk as a Southern gentleman, calling a lady "ma'am." And then lose his temper and call guests unseemly names. He was a night owl, who was terrified of not being able to sleep and would end up taking prescription pills just to do that, and consume more to wake up again.

In later 1974, things began unraveling for Elvis. Even though Elvis did not like the idea of his father remarrying after his mother's death, he was upset that Vernon and his stepmother Dee separated. At the same time, Elvis's own relationship with Linda Thompson had also come to a close. As two sensitive, close, and spiritual people, it was difficult for Elvis to let go of Thompson.

In addition, Elvis's long-term pianist, David Briggs, had enough and wanted to return back to Nashville, to the studios.

Perhaps compensating for his losses at this time, Elvis's weight ballooned. When his regular band members saw him around this time, after a while apart, they noticed the dramatic increase and how it changed Elvis's appearance remarkably.

Tony Brown, his new pianist, recalls the moment Elvis arrived, "He fell out of the limousine to his knees. People jumped to help and he pushed them away, like, 'Don't help me!' He always did that when he fell. He walked onstage and held on to the mike for the first thirty minutes like it was a post. Everybody was scared."

Elvis Presley with girlfriend Linda Thompson, 1976

Elvis struggled with relationships and his weight ballooned

Elvis's guitarist in the band, John Wilkinson, watched on too: "The lights went down and Elvis came up the stairs. He was all gut. He was slurring. He was so f*****d up. It was obvious he was drugged, that there was something terribly wrong with his body. It was so bad, the words to the songs were barely intelligible. He could barely get through the introductions. We were in a state of shock. I remember crying. He cut the show short, yet it seemed like it went on forever."

Elvis began to look more and more weary onstage, 1975

Things got mildly better for the next three nights of the tour, where he showed more enthusiasm and seemed to be more with it. However, it wasn't long before it worsened again, and when they were in Detroit for another show, Wilkinson recalled, "I watched him in his dressing room, just draped over a chair, unable to move. So often I thought, 'Boss, why don't you just cancel this tour and take a year off?' I mentioned something once in a guarded moment. He patted me on the back and said, 'It'll be alright. Don't worry about it.'"

His tour continued, relentlessly, and Elvis went through the motions, performing one city a day. In 1975, things did not get better for Elvis. While he should have celebrated turning forty on January 8, instead he lamented he was getting old, worrying about his age.

By now, Elvis's doctor, whose name Elvis shortened from Dr. George Nichopoulos to simply Dr. Nick, would have concerns over Elvis's health.

Just twenty days after his birthday, he was admitted to the hospital for an enlarged colon and a detoxification. Nichopoulos kept Elvis in for what was to be several days, but they found more problems on his arrival. In addition to the enlarged colon and detox, Elvis had a biopsy on his liver, which showed he had quite severe damage. According to the attending physicians, it was due to drug abuse.

A rare, untroubled smile from Elvis

Nichopoulos had said the colon problem was caused by bad diet, mainly The King's love of fried food and sugar. In order to overcome the damage to both, he needed to change his diet and stop taking the pills.

Normally, Elvis took the winter holidays off and started work after his birthday each year. But in 1975, he had agreed to a New Year's Eve performance, to 80,000 people in Michigan. According to reports, his financial woes were worsening, and despite all the extravagances and the record earnings of his Vegas and concert years, Elvis had borrowed against Graceland and needed the money.

To everyone involved in the performance, it was not his finest.

It seemed the different arrangements and layout of the band and staging was not communicated and so Elvis was not best prepared. It was freezing. Wilkinson said, "The trumpet players' lips were so cold they could barely blow their horns. It was so cold our strings kept changing key. Oh, we were glad to get out of there."

Elvis's famous bad temper got the better of him. He apparently shouted at everyone on the way back home, and was furious at how it unraveled.

Parker, however, had managed to secure $800,000, understood to be another record for the takings of one artist at the time, for one night's performance. At this time, Parker had also made another lucrative deal Elvis could not refuse. For $5.4 million, he sold off the rights to RCA for all material recorded by Elvis up to 1972, amounting to over 350 tracks and fifty albums.

By 1976, things were getting out of control.

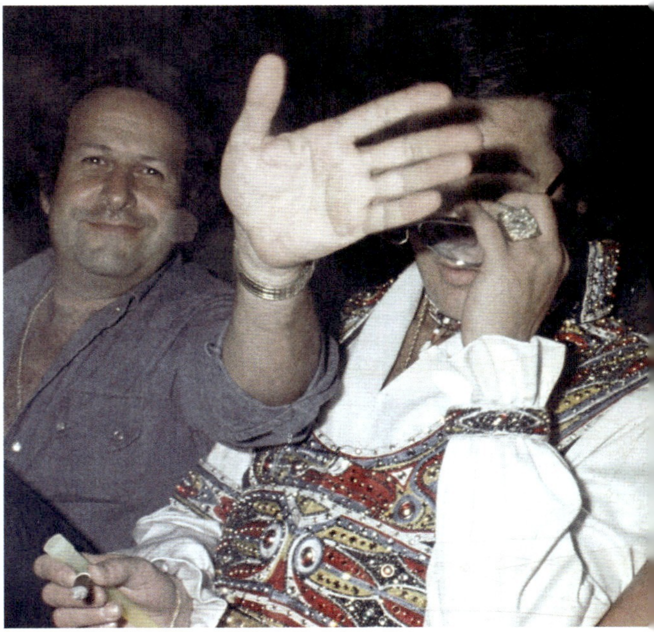

Elvis and his road manager, Joe Esposito, depart for another concert

Elvis performing live with guitarist James Burton

Live in Las Vegas, 1975

Elvis strides around a ranch on set with a gun in his hand.

Under pressure from RCA to record more material, which had previously managed three albums annually, Elvis refused to go back to the studios in Nashville. RCA asked for Hollywood or Memphis. He refused.

Unbelievably, RCA were so desperate for Elvis to record new songs that they sent a reported $200,000 worth of recording equipment to Elvis, at Graceland. They even flew his band from Los Angeles and studio executives from Nashville to join him at Graceland. The band and the team waited for Elvis to join them in the den at Graceland. It hit midnight, and still there was no Elvis. Then word came that Elvis was sick and a doctor was seeing to him.

There was a different version of events of this particular night, as told by Elvis's close companions and bodyguards, Red and Sonny West and Dave Hebler. They told their story in a book called *Elvis: What Happened?*, a tell-all book that was published just weeks before his death.

Much has been said of this book, and others that followed from the supposed loyal friends of the Memphis Mafia, in particular whether the authors were merely disgruntled ex-employees or were sharing the truth. According to the Wests and Hebler, Elvis was upstairs in his room, surrounded by automatic weapons, pistols, rifles, and rockets. Many have recalled Elvis's obsession with guns and weaponry, and that he had a collection later in life.

Red West claimed Elvis handed him a list of names and photographs of people that had been shared by the Memphis police, and that "Elvis had it all planned. He wanted myself and Dave Hebler and Dick Grob, the former cop [who had gone to work for Elvis some years earlier], to go out and lure them, and he said he was going to kill them."

Elvis performing in concert at the Philadelphia Spectrum in 1976

In the book, they describe Elvis sharing with them that the recording sessions would be his cover and he could sneak out of the house and return quickly to Graceland. After moving him off the topic, the recording session finally began.

It was not a particularly productive or exciting session. Elvis recorded just twelve songs over a week. Compared with *Elvis is Back!*, it was a big disappointment.

The album *From Elvis Presley Boulevard* featured ten of the songs recorded. Reviews were lukewarm, with his delivery sufficient but not exciting.

From 1975 to his death in 1977, Elvis's albums did not top the charts. However, five albums made the country charts, coming in the top five. *Promised Land* (1975), *From Elvis Presley Boulevard* (1976), and *Moody Blue* (1977) were all Number One on the country charts. Elvis's music had returned to its beginnings.

His singles still had the attention of modern radio though, with eight singles from this era hitting the top ten of the contemporary charts. *My Boy* was a Number One in the adult contemporary category and "Moody Blue" hit the number two spot.

Word from those RCA Graceland sessions was that Elvis was skittish and prone to big mood swings, going from indifference to satisfaction to crazy. At one point, he apparently pointed a gun at the speakers and had to have the gun forcibly removed from him and the session canceled.

Elvis Presley performs in concert at the Milwaukee Arena on April 27, 1977

Elvis's ex-girlfriend, Linda Thompson's Birthday Party at Gatsby's—March 23, 1977

In early 1977, despite the hero worship of Elvis in the cities he toured, Elvis was barely delivering an average performance. Some shows were good, some were average, and some were awful. Some were even more critical of him at this time, with the journalist Tony Scherman writing, "Elvis Presley had become a grotesque caricature of his sleek, energetic former self. Hugely overweight, his mind dulled by the pharmacopoeia he daily ingested, he was barely able to pull himself through his abbreviated concerts."

In Louisiana, on March 31, Elvis was a no-show. After calling his hotel room and waiting, the show was canceled; the audience was told Elvis was sick.

Checked in again at the Baptist Hospital under the care of Nichopoulos, Elvis was in fact sick. The press was informed he was being treated for exhaustion. In fact, he had been abusing uppers, continued a bad diet, refused to exercise, and was not sleeping.

There was cause for concern. He had been using prescription pills every day over the past two years and now he was taking them in random doses that were putting him at risk of overdose. Linda Thompson recalls him being unconscious a number of times.

Nichopoulos was by now Elvis's only physician, apparently organized so that the doctor could keep a close eye on his patient and know exactly what was prescribed and how much. It seemed a better solution than prescriptions coming from a variety of doctors, with no way of knowing how much and what drugs he was ingesting.

While Elvis was in some degree of denial, considering his pills as medicine, he also was aware they made him feel good.

Elvis sings a ballad in one of his last shows in 1977

While Nichopoulos's argument that he could start to wean Elvis off the prescription drugs was a good one, it was brought into question when it was discovered after Elvis's death that he had prescribed his patient an average of 25 pills a day, totaling 5,300 in a short seven-month period.

Elvis checked himself out of hospital after five days. Elvis's last week was unremarkable. He saw friends, spoke to them on the telephone, and played racquetball. He watched gospel shows on television.

He spent time with Ginger Alden, his last girlfriend. He read the Bible, ate cheeseburgers, and took his pills.

On August 15, 1977 Elvis woke at four p.m., ate breakfast, and played with Lisa Marie on the lawn, watching and laughing as she raced around in her electric cart.

Elvis requested an appointment with his dentist at ten-thirty p.m. that same night. His dentist, Dr. Lester Hofman, saw Elvis and met Alden for the first time. He x-rayed her teeth and gave Elvis two fillings.

Back home at Graceland, Elvis apparently called his doctor to ask for more painkillers, because of the fillings. Elvis talked about his concert playlist with one of his security men who said he told him, "We'll make this tour the best ever."

Elvis then changed to go and play racquetball again in the early hours of the morning, this time with his cousin Billy Smith and his wife, Jo. As was customary at this time, Elvis and Alden went to bed at around four a.m. Around half an hour later, Elvis sat at a piano and played some gospel numbers.

At nine a.m. the same morning, August 16, Alden woke to find Elvis still reading.

Telling her he was going into the bathroom to read, as he could not sleep, she warned him "Okay, just don't fall asleep."

Dancing erratically with his guitar onstage in 1977

Elvis Presley in Hawaii with Ginger Alden, March 1977

Death and Legacy

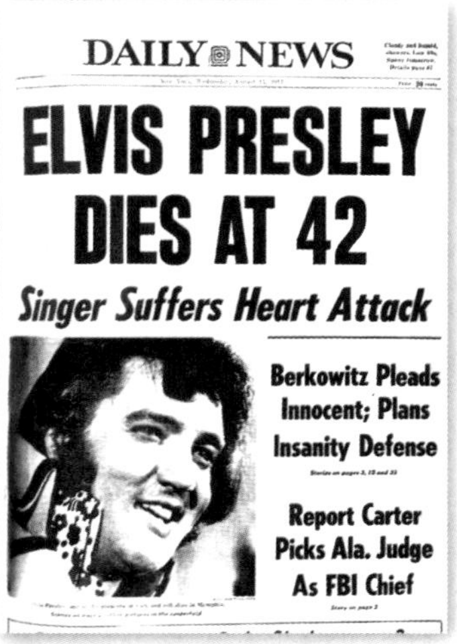

DAILY NEWS

ELVIS PRESLEY DIES AT 42

Singer Suffers Heart Attack

Berkowitz Pleads Innocent; Plans Insanity Defense

Report Carter Picks Ala. Judge As FBI Chief

Front page of the Daily News *dated August 17, 1977*

Elvis's premature and controversial death and long-lasting legacy

Elvis told his girlfriend, Ginger Alden, he was going into the bathroom to try to sleep; she later said she knew he was going into the bathroom to take more pills.

At this point, it was likely to be the third round of pills he had taken in six hours. According to the medical examiner later, as many as ten different types of prescription pills were found in his system, including Codeine, Ethinamate, Methaqualone, barbiturates, Placidyl, Valium, Demerol, Meperidine, Morphine, Chloropheniramine, and antihistamines.

At one-thirty p.m. Alden woke and knocked on the bathroom door. Hearing no reply, she went in and found his body slumped on the floor in front of the toilet.

Alden screamed for help and Al Strada and Joe Esposito rushed to her aid and called the fire department. With an ambulance racing to the scene, Elvis's daughter Lisa Marie and his father Vernon came in to see what was wrong.

Lisa Marie was rushed out of the bathroom, but not before she apparently cried out "What's wrong with my daddy? Something's wrong with my daddy, and I'm going to find out."

A few hours later, at four p.m. Elvis's father Vernon greeted reporters on the steps of Graceland and told them, "My son is dead."

The King of Rock 'n' Roll was dead.

It was hard to believe that only a couple of months before, on June 25, he had delivered his last live show.

Those around him at the time recalled he was mortified that his previously loyal close family and friends, three of his bodyguards who were sacked by Vernon, would release the gossipy, tell-all book *Elvis: What Happened?* He had apparently attempted to stop its release by offering money to the publishers of the book.

The book was released in the United States just four days before he died.

An artistic tribute at a memorial service for Elvis Presley, August 1977

A young man in an "Elvis RIP" T-shirt attends a memorial service for Elvis Presley, August 1977

While the family decided to keep the autopsy report private, it was later revealed that Elvis had died of heart failure and had an enlarged liver and advanced arteriosclerosis.

The autopsy report has been challenged many times, and was reopened again in 1994, where the Coroner Dr. Joseph Davis determined, "There is nothing in any of the data that supports a death from drugs. In fact, everything points to a sudden, violent heart attack.

"Whether or not combined drug intoxication was in fact the cause, there is little doubt that polypharmacy contributed significantly to Presley's premature death."

Award-winning Elvis biographer Guralnick, however, states of Elvis's death, "Drug use was heavily implicated. No one ruled out the possibility of anaphylactic shock brought on by the codeine pills . . . to which he was known to have had a mild allergy."

More reports and speculation followed, and as historian and pathologist Michael Baden states, "Elvis had had an enlarged heart for a long time. That, together with his drug habit, caused his death. But he was difficult to diagnose; it was a judgment call."

After medical examiners discovered the volume of prescriptions given to Elvis, the Tennessee Board of Medical Examiners charged Nichopoulos with being criminally liable for his death and indiscriminate, although he was later acquitted of the charges. His license was suspended for three months and was later permanently revoked after the same Tennessee Medical Board brought new charges of over-prescription.

Thousands of fans and press had gathered at Graceland, mourning the loss of their rock 'n' roll King.

Two days after his passing, on August 18, Elvis Presley's funeral was held at Graceland with an open casket. With near hysteria building amongst fans who had gathered at the gates, on the day of his funeral, two women were killed, and a third seriously injured, after a car drove into a group of fans.

The funeral of Elvis Presley in Memphis, Tennessee

After the funeral, a long procession to the cemetery went past 80,000 people.

He was buried in a mausoleum, at the Forest Hill Cemetery in Memphis.

Then President of the United States, Jimmy Carter, issued a statement:

"Elvis Presley's death deprives our country of a part of itself. He was unique, irreplaceable. More than twenty years ago, he burst upon the scene with an impact that was unprecedented and will probably never be equaled. His music and his personality, fusing the styles of white country and black rhythm and blues, permanently changed the face of American popular culture. His following was immense. And he was a symbol to people the world over of the vitality, rebelliousness, and good humor of this country."

Later, one of Elvis's cousins, Billy Mann, provided the *National Enquirer* with a photograph of the open casket, after accepting $18,000 for it. It was reportedly the *Enquirer*'s biggest selling issue ever.

Even Elvis's girlfriend Ginger Alden succumbed to the lure of a $105,000 deal with the *Enquirer* in return for telling her story. However, she apparently settled for less on breaking the exclusivity arrangement she had signed with the *Enquirer*.

Police officers on motorcycles escort a white hearse containing the body of American rock and roll singer Elvis Presley

THE COMMERCIAL APPEAL

Death Captures Crown Of Rock And Roll —Elvis Dies Apparently After Heart Attack

Elvis Went From Rags To Riches

Hearse Takes Body Of Elvis Presley From Baptist Hospital

'Are You Sure There's No Mistake?' —The Desired Answer Never Came

View of the front page of the Commercial Appeal newspaper the day after the death of Elvis Presley

Memphis Press-Scimitar

SPECIAL EDITION

Memphis Leads the World in Mourning the Monarch of Rock 'n Roll

A Lonely Life Ends on Elvis Presley Boulevard

A Tribute to Elvis

Mourners In Waiting For Last Homecoming Of Revered Singer

View of the front page of the Memphis Press-Scimitar *newspaper the day after the death of Elvis Presley*

Elvis continued to top the charts, even after his death. "Way Down" reached the top of the country charts only a few days after his funeral and burial.

As crazed fans attempted to break into the mausoleum, in October Vernon agreed to move his body. Elvis and his mother were exhumed and buried again, this time in the Meditation Garden at Graceland.

With a so many people involved in Elvis's life, his Last Will and Testament brought a lot of attention. Originally, Lisa Marie, Vernon, and Elvis's grandmother Minnie Mae were to inherit Elvis's estate. Interestingly, neither Priscilla nor any of his romantic loves were included and did not stand to inherit anything from Elvis's estate.

Elvis Presley's funeral cortege in Memphis, Tennessee on August 18, 1977

FREE
CAR
WASH

Along with witnesses Charles F. Hodge and Ann Dewey Smith, Ginger Alden was a third witness and signatory on his Will.

(b) After payment of all expenses, taxes and costs incurred in the management of the expenses, taxes and costs incurred in the management of the trust estate, the Trustee is authorized to accumulate the net income or to pay or apply so much of the net income and such portion of the principal at any time and from time to time to time for health, education, support, comfortable maintenance and welfare of: (1) My daughter, Lisa Marie Presley, and any other lawful issue I might have, (2) my grandmother, Minnie Mae Presley, (3) my father, Vernon E. Presley, and (4) such other relatives of mine living at the time of my death who in the absolute discretion of my Trustees are in need of emergency assistance for any of the above mentioned purposes and the Trustee is able to make such distribution without affecting the ability of the trust to meet the present needs of the first three numbered categories of beneficiaries herein mentioned or to meet the reasonably expected future needs of the first three classes of beneficiaries herein mentioned. Any decision of the Trustee as to whether or not distribution, to any of the persons described hereunder shall be final and conclusive and not subject to question by any legatee or beneficiary hereunder.

(c) Upon the death of my Father, Vernon E. Presley, the Trustee is instructed to make no further distributions to the fourth category of beneficiaries and such beneficiaries shall cease to have any interest whatsoever in this trust.

(d) Upon the death of both my said father and my said grandmother, the Trustee is directed to divide the Residuary Trust into separate and equal trusts, creating one such equal trust for each of my lawful children then surviving and one such equal trust for the living issue collectively, if any, of any deceased child of mine. The share, if any, for the issue of any such deceased child, shall immediately vest in such issue in equal shares but shall be subject to the provisions of Item V herein. Separate books and records shall be kept for each trust, but it shall not be necessary that a physical division of the assets be made as to each trust.

An excerpt from The Last Will and Testament of Elvis A. Presley

Lisa Marie Presley inherited her father's estate

His father, Vernon, was provided for in his will

Despite a very clear, legally binding Will, there was speculation and dispute over the estate years later, closing in 1983. Almost two years after Elvis's death, his father Vernon passed away, joining his first wife and child to be buried in the Meditation Garden at Graceland. After the death of Minnie Mae, the estate was passed in full to Lisa Marie. She would not stand to access the estate and the funds until she was twenty-five years of age, however.

Valued at $4.9 million in 1979, the estate was too expensive to run. It was reportedly estimated that it would take half a million dollars a year to run Graceland.

After court battles over the estate, brought about by lawsuits, it was agreed that Parker should turn over his interest from Elvis's recordings (both audio and video), to RCA and to the Presleys for a monetary settlement.

Lisa Marie was granted a court-appointed guardian ad litem, to help manage the estate and review its financial affairs. He reported that Parker "handled affairs not in Elvis's but in his own best interest."

Priscilla was advised by the court to sell Graceland in order to avoid bankruptcy. Instead, in 1982 she arranged for Graceland to be opened to the public for tours. With the huge interest from the public and the fascination with Elvis's private life, it continues to be open today. Through Priscilla's shrewdness, and solid business decisions, she increased its worth over the years to be over $100 million by the mid-1990s. By the millennium, Graceland had brought in $100 million into the Memphis local economy as well.

Fans walk by the entrance to Graceland, the home of Elvis Presley

Elvis Presley's grave at Graceland

ELVIS
AARON
PRESLEY
JANUARY 8, 1935
AUGUST 16, 1977
VERNON ELVIS PRESLEY
I Love you

The Graceland home is close to, although not exactly, as Elvis left it. And the second floor, where his bedroom is located, is not available to tour and remains closed off.

Graceland was added to the National Register of Historic Places in 1991 and a National Historic Landmark in 2006. In 1993, Graceland purchased the shopping center plaza that was built across the road in the 60s. The shops and attractions there are now known as Graceland Plaza.

The Graceland property is still owned by Lisa Marie, along with her father's personal effects. She sold 85 percent of the business of Elvis's estate in 2005, to an entertainment company, of which her mother Priscilla retains a seat on the board of directors. She owns the remaining 15 percent.

In addition to managing the estate, Priscilla also pushed for state law to guarantee the rights over deceased celebrity images. As such, Elvis Presley Enterprises Inc (EPE) now owns the rights to the name Elvis Presley and any merchandise created and sold in the US must pay royalties to EPE in advance.

From 1979, the EPE business has brought hundreds of lawsuits on people or businesses distributing or using the King's images without their permission.

The interest in Elvis Presley lives on. In addition to websites and online blogs written about The King of Rock 'n' Roll, hundreds of books have been published and the Graceland mansion is the second most visited home in America by tourists, after the White House.

We Love You Tender *book launch, 1980*

Priscilla Presley and Lisa Marie Presley shortly after Elvis's death

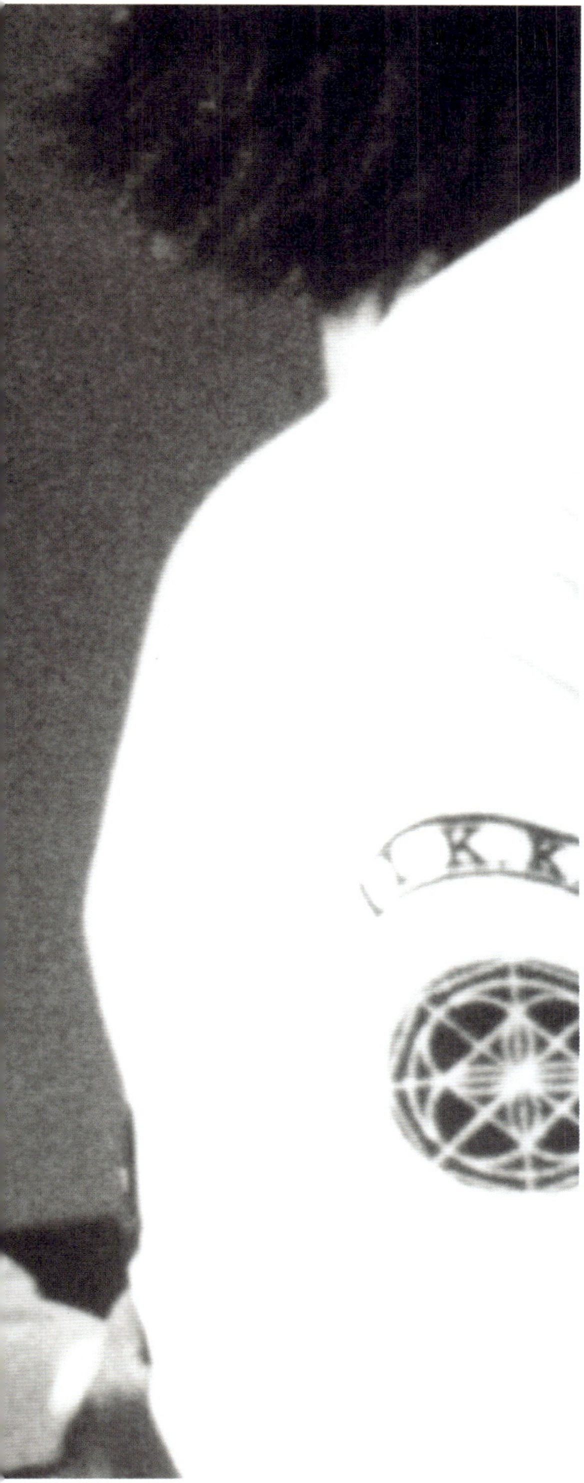

Elvis's albums and songs have been reissued, remastered, and repackaged countless times, and will continue to sell. His legacy is enormous and wide reaching.

From 1977 until 1981, six singles of Elvis's were released and went on to become top ten hits on the country charts. Elvis has been inducted into four musical halls of fame, including the Rock and Roll Hall of Fame in 1986, the country Music Hall of Fame in 1998, the Gospel Music Hall of Fame in 2001, and the Rockabilly Hall of Fame in 2007. He was awarded the Blues Foundation's WC Handy Award in 1984, the Academy of country Music's first Golden Hat Award, and the American Music Award's 1987 Award of Merit.

His music is still relevant today and will no doubt continue to be in future. For 2002's World Cup soccer advertising campaign, Nike used a remix of Elvis's "A Little Less Conversation," by Junkie XL (titled Elvis Vs XL), and it went on to top the charts in over 20 countries. In 2003, a remix of "Rubberneckin" (from 1969) topped the US chart. The following year the Elvis 50th Anniversary release of "That's All Right" also topped the US chart.

In 2005, three singles of Elvis's, "Jailhouse Rock," "One Night," and "It's Now or Never" went to Number One in the United Kingdom. Of the seventeen singles issued that year, each hit the UK's top five.

In the early and second half of 2000 to 2010, Elvis ranked in the highest income earners. The year of his seventy-fifth birthday, 2010, *Viva Elvis: The Album* was released, with his vocals added to new instrumental recordings of his songs. He ranked second on *Forbes* list that year, with an income of $60 million. By 2011, there were 15,000 licensed Elvis products.

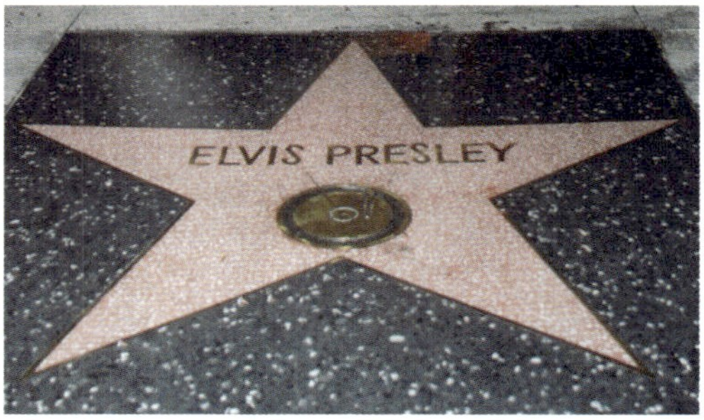

The star of Elvis Presley on the Hollywood Walk of Fame

A still from the film This Is Elvis *released in 1981*

Incredibly, Elvis continues to hold the record for the most songs ever charted on Billboard's Top 40 and Top 100. Joel Whitburn, chart statistician, announced that Elvis's total was 104 and 151 songs on those charts, respectively. Other biographers and historians have recorded slightly different amounts, but all declare he had over 100 songs on both charts.

Elvis Presley receives a platinum record from a man commemorating his live album As Recorded at Madison Square Garden *selling 1 million copies*

Elvis also holds the record for having eighty cumulative weeks at Number One. He also still holds the records for the most Number One hits and Top Ten hits in the UK, with twenty-one and seventy-six respectively.

Elvis had achieved what many would have declared impossible. He made a return from two years out of the limelight while serving for the Army, breaking new records. He returned from soft, fluffy movies and the critics' dismissal of him to make a comeback that broke new records again.

He filled Madison Square Garden for four consecutive shows, breaking every attendance and box office record. He broke ground by reaching a billion people live (and on delay) with his 1971 Aloha From Hawaii satellite show. He even won a Golden Globe for *Elvis on Tour* and a Gospel Award Grammy for *He Touched Me*.

Elvis continues to have fans worldwide, and some are fanatical about Elvis's death, believing it was a hoax—that it was faked so he may retire in peace.

Still today, there are reported sightings of Elvis that hit the newsstands and media. The theory surrounding this "fake death" is based on discrepancies on his death certificate and accounts from those claiming he was planning it to avoid continued attention.

For many other fans, Elvis lives on in the nightly shows audiences can take in along The Strip in Las Vegas. For some, being an Elvis impersonator means making a good living.

There are estimated to be over 80,000 Elvis impersonators globally, although it is difficult to substantiate this number. The Elvis impersonator is such a well developed category now that it is considered there are three main types of impersonator, including the look-alikes, who focus on Elvis's fashions and look, the sound-alikes, who focus on their vocal impressions of Elvis singing and talking, and the impersonators who are a combination of the two. Elvis impersonators provide a source of fascination on their own and movies such as *Elvis* and *3000 Miles to Graceland* have been produced on the topic.

Elvis Presley during a live performance of 'Aloha from Hawaii'

Opposite page: Elvis Presley onstage singing in performance at Madison Square Garden, 1972

In addition to his posthumous success and continued fan worship, Elvis's legacy lives on in the music world. Some of the world's most exciting musicians and singers have attributed their musical influence to Elvis Presley. Ranging from blues artists, to country and rock bands, Elvis's impression and inspiration has been astonishing.

"Elvis is the greatest cultural force in the twentieth century. He introduced the beat to everything, music, language, clothes, it's a whole new social revolution—the 60's comes from it."

—Leonard Bernstein

"When I first heard Elvis's voice, I just knew that I wasn't going to work for anybody; and nobody was going to be my boss . . . He is the deity supreme of rock and roll religion as it exists in today's form. Hearing him for the first time was like busting out of jail—I thank God for Elvis Presley."

—Bob Dylan

Bob Dylan

"The highlight of my career? That's easy, Elvis recording one of my songs."

—Bob Dylan

"There have been a lotta tough guys. There have been pretenders. And there have been contenders. But there is only one king."

". . . it was like he came along and whispered some dream in everybody's ear, and somehow we all dreamed it."

—Bruce Springsteen

"A lot has been written and said about why he was so great, but I think the best way to appreciate his greatness is just to go back and play some of the old records . . . Time has a way of being very unkind to old records, but Elvis's keep getting better and better."

—Huey Lewis

"Elvis was the king. No doubt about it. People like myself, Mick Jagger, and all the others only followed in his footsteps."

—Rod Stewart

"Before Elvis, there was nothing."

—John Lennon

John Lennon

Roy Orbison

"I wasn't just a fan, I was his brother. He said I was good and I said he was good; we never argued about that. Elvis was a hard worker, dedicated, and God loved him. Last time I saw him was at Graceland. We sang "Old Blind Barnabus" together, a gospel song. I love him and hope to see him in heaven. There'll never be another like that soul brother."

—James Brown

"He was a unique artist—an original in an area of imitators."

—Mick Jagger

"Ask anyone. If it hadn't been for Elvis, I don't know where popular music would be. He was the one that started it all off, and he was definitely the start of it for me."

"It was Elvis that got me interested in music. I've been an Elvis fan since I was a kid."

—Elton John

"When we were kids growing up in Liverpool, all we ever wanted to be was Elvis Presley."

—Paul McCartney

"Elvis is a major hero of mine. I was probably stupid enough to believe that having the same birthday as him actually meant something."

—David Bowie

The influence and effect Elvis Presley had on his fans is immense. But Elvis also moved modern culture and lifestyle in a new direction. He broke rules of what was previously declared black and white, male and female, un-Christian and Christian. He pushed and challenged boundaries across racial, gender, sexual, and religious attitudes.

To describe him as The King of Rock 'n' Roll was almost too narrow a label, for his impact on fashion, cinema, music—across rock, country, blues, and pop, as well as his role in crossing racial boundaries and prejudice, was evident in the progression of popular American culture during and since his reign.

Elvis Presley was a true rebel—he did things his way and in doing so, paved the way for new talent, and new cultural and social thinking.

"He was the firstest with the mostest."

—Roy Orbison

James Brown

Iconic Elvis during his '68 Comeback Special

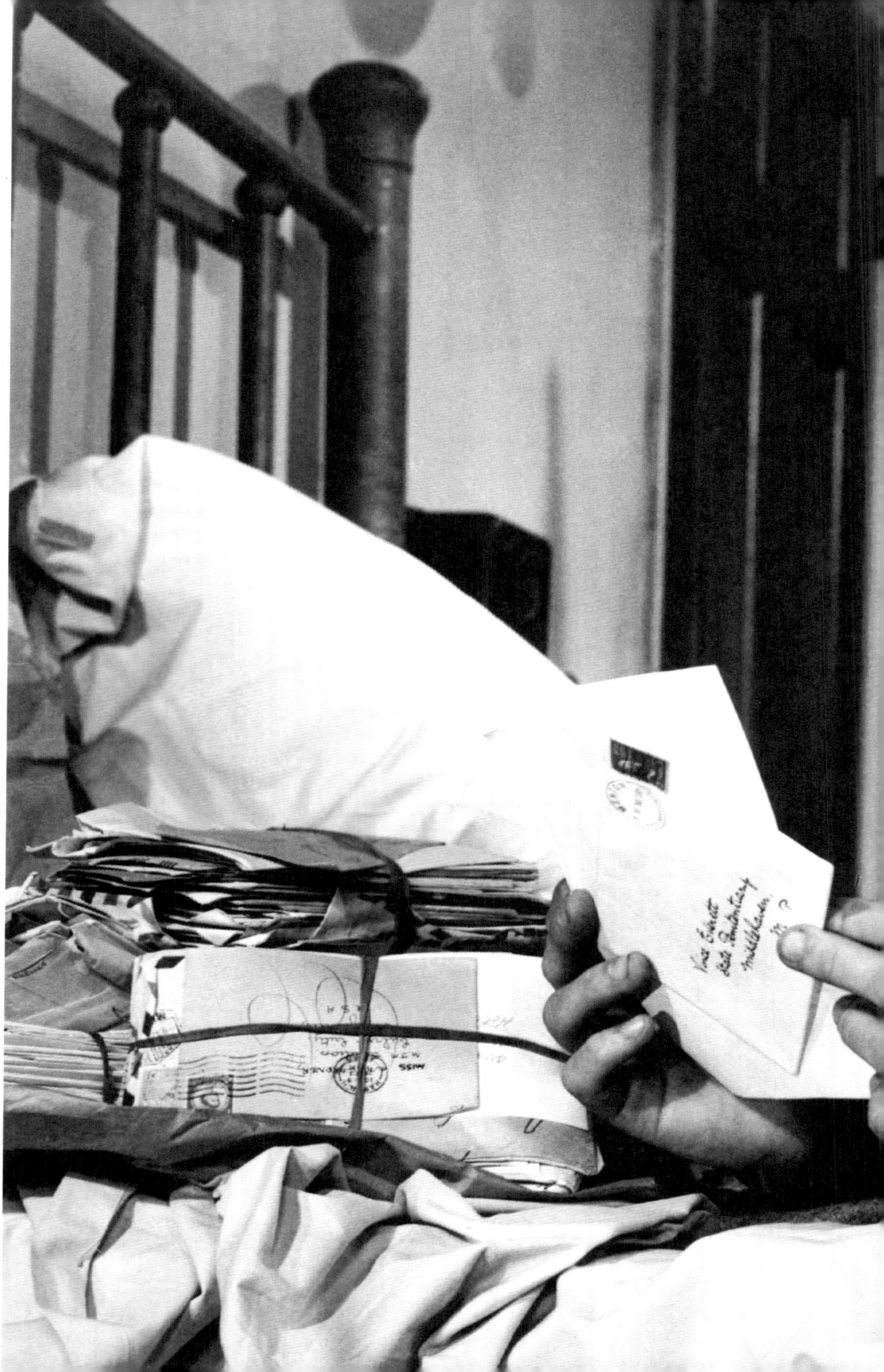

Elvis Presley stretched out on the bed reading some letters in a scene from the movie Jailhouse Rock.

Index

Picture Credits

All images featured in this book are courtesy of Getty Images © Getty Images.

Page 230—Waring Abbott/Michael Ochs Archives/Getty Images

Pages 238–239—Ron Galella/WireImage/Getty Images